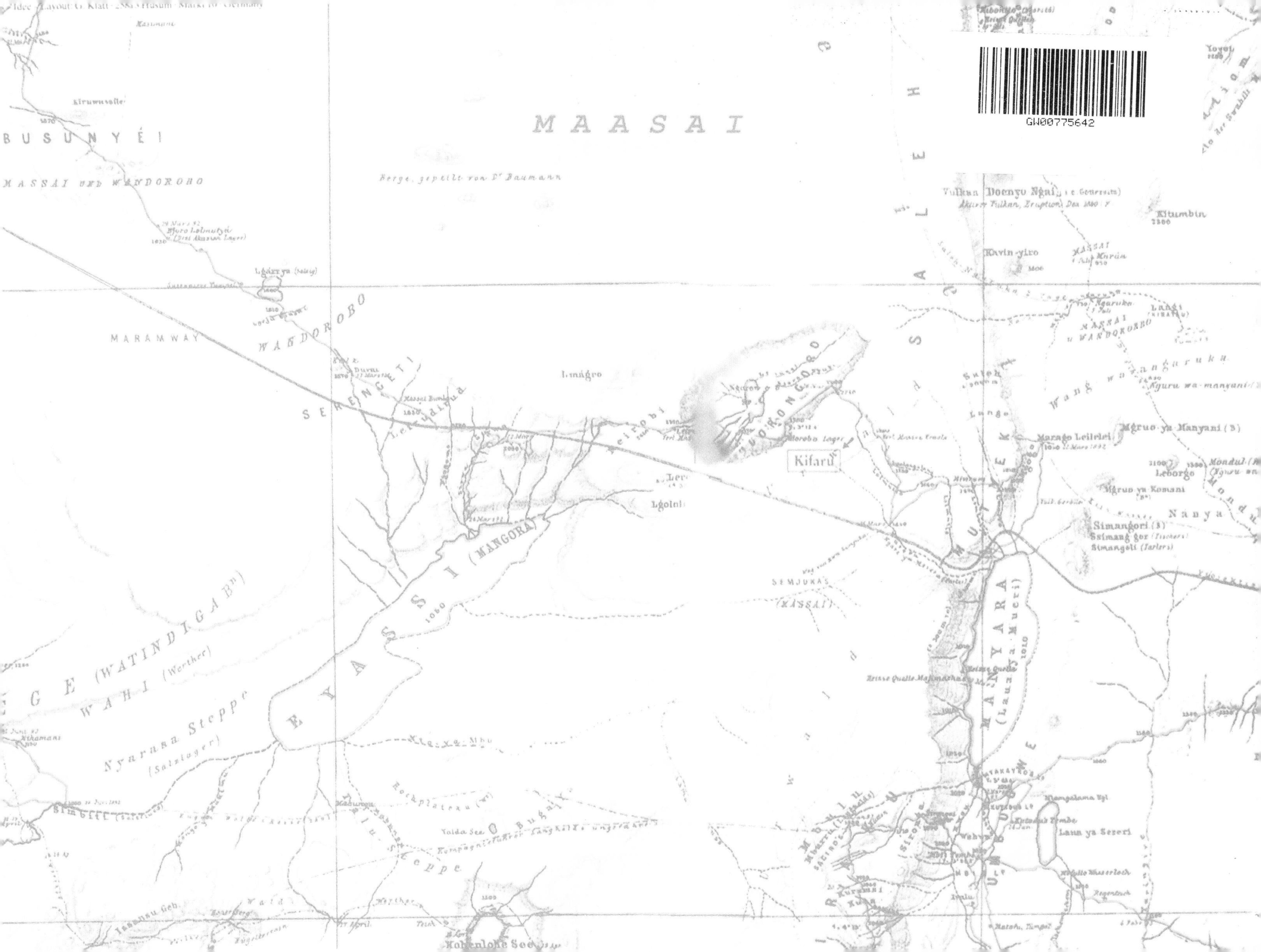

MAASAI

BUSUNYÉI

MASSAI UND WANDOROBO

MARAMWAY

WANDOROBO

SERENGETI

EYASSI (MANGORA)

GE (WATINDIGA?)

WAHI (Werther)

Nyarasa Steppe
(Salzlager)

Berge, gepeilt von Dr Baumann

Lenágro

NGORONGORO

Kifaru

Vulkan Doenyo Ngai (? Gottessitz)
Aktiver Vulkan, Eruption Dez 1880 ?

Kitumbin

Kavin-yiro

MASSAI
u WANDOROBO

Wang wa manguruka

Mgruo ya Manyani (B)

Marago Leileli

Leborgo

Mondul

Mgruo ya Komani

Simangori (B)

Nabya

St MJUKAS
(KASSAI)

MANYARA
(Laua ya Mueri)

Yaida See

Rockplateau

Nyarasa Steppe

KKie X & Mbo

Laua ya Sezeri

Hohenlohe See

# The Ngorongoro Story

Tom Lithgow • Hugo van Lawick

*Camerapix Publishers International*

N A I R O B I

*November 1931*

*Professor Hans Reck and Ray Hewlett (game warden, right), in November 1931, with two lions which were shot after attacking the Olduvai excavations team.*

2

*Map of the Ngorongoro Conservation Area.*

# The Ngorongoro Story

*The Lerai Forest, and Lake Magadi behind it, add texture to the broad floor of the Ngorongoro Crater.*

*Julius Kambarage Nyerere, President of Tanzania 1961–1985*

# THE PRESIDENT'S MESSAGE

Declaration by the late president of Tanzania, Dr J Nyerere, and signed by him and two of his ministers at the International Fauna and Flora Conference in Arusha in 1961:

*'The survival of our wildlife is a matter of great concern to us all in Africa. These wild creatures and the wild places they inhabit are not only important as a source of wonder and inspiration, but are an integral part of our natural resources and our future livelihood and well-being.*

*'In accepting the trusteeship of our wildlife, we solemnly declare that we will do everything in our power to make sure that our children's grandchildren will be able to enjoy this rich and precious heritage.*

*'The conservation of wildlife and wild places calls for specialist knowledge, trained manpower, and money, and we look to other nations to help us in this important task – the success or failure of which not only affects the continent of Africa but the rest of the world as well.'*

# DEDICATION

This book is dedicated to the memory of Adolf Siedentopf, 1872–1932: explorer, farmer, prospector, chemist, and naturalist, known as 'the feared, unapproachable King of the Ngorongoro'.

Adolf Siedentopf, 1872–1932

# CONTENTS

# ACKNOWLEDGMENTS

It is impossible to write any book involving years of research without the assistance of many people. This book is no exception to the rule.

The late Henry Fosbrooke, first conservator of the Ngorongoro Conservation Area (1959 to 1965), was an able guide and adviser.

The two most valuable contacts who assisted in establishing the background and life of Adolf Siedentopf were the late Ursula Oetker, the niece of Adolf's wife, Paula, and the late Eva Wenkel, former companion to Paula Siedentopf at the crater in the days before the First World War.

I am indebted to the late Mary Leakey for her kind assistance with the chapter on the prehistoric grave finds in the crater.

The late Solomon ole Saibull, who succeeded Henry Fosbrooke as conservator and who was himself a Maasai, was extremely helpful with the preparation and the editing of the Maasai chapter. A member of the laiser clan and non-practising member of the laibonok subclan, Solomon served on many committees, where his experience and knowledge were in great demand.

*The late Solomon Ole Saibull, who succeded Henry Fosbrooke as conservator of the Ngorongoro Conservation Area.*

The remoteness of my farm near the crater, over a hundred miles from the nearest secretarial services in Arusha, made the typing assistance volunteered by my next-door neighbour and very special friend, Margaret Gibb (now Kullender), absolutely invaluable.

It would have been impossible for me to cope with this book without the assistance of my Austrian wife, Gudrun. She translated most of the German text used in the research, and was always at hand to encourage and assist. Whilst I was floundering around in the literary forest of research my daughter, Catherine, sorted out the individual 'trees', and was indispensable assisting with the final manuscript.

My two sons, Tom and Alexander, have also joined in with the family scrum down to help launch this book.

One of Africa's leading photographers, and a good friend, the late Hugo van Lawick was a great help and encouragement with his ideas. He suffered for many years from acute emphysema, and used the last of his energies completing a superlative wildlife movie, so was unable to provide all the photos for my book. Hugo's support and encouragement provided the necessary stimulus for me to roll up my sleeves and complete the manuscript which I had started fifty years ago!

I would like to acknowledge the assistance of Tanzanian governments, past and present, and the Ngorongoro Conservation Area Authority.

Finally I have been grateful for the invaluable patience and expertise of Rukhsana Haq, John Dawson, and the publishers, Camerapix, in bringing this project to completion.

*Plaque commemorating Mary Leakey's discovery, in 1959, of the skull of Australopithecus boisei, believed to have roamed the area around Olduvai Gorge almost two million years ago.*

This book was designed and produced by
Camerapix Publishers International
P.O. Box 45048
Nairobi 00100, GPO
Kenya
E-mail: camerapix@iconnect.co.ke

© Camerapix 2004

ISBN: 1-904722-04-0

Text: Tom Lithgow
Photography: Hugo van Lawick, David Pluth, and Camerapix
Production Director: Rukhsana Haq
Design: Shakira Ahmed
Editor: John Dawson

**Picture Credits:**
*Camerapix:* 4,5,17,18,19,24,25,26,33(left and right), 36,37,39,40,41,47,49,
50(left and right),51,55,69,72,75,77,80,81,83,87,89,94(below),112,114,118,125,
129,139

*Tom Lithgow:* 2,6,8,10,12,13,23,27,28,43,45,53,59,60,61,62,63,64(right),68,143

*Hugo Van Lewick:* 29,38,46,74,79,82,84 (above and below), 85,86,90, 91,
94 (above),96,99,100,101,105,107,110-111, 113,115,116,117,119,121,131,133,
136,137,138(above),140,141(above and below)

*David Pluth:* 9,14,15,20-21,22,31,32(left and right),35,52,56,57,70,71,78,
88,93,95,97,98,103,104,108,122,127,128,130,132,135,138(below),142

*David Bygott:* 58,64 (above left and below), 67,76 (above and below),
123 (above and below)

5. Eine Trägerkarawane bringt Vorräte von Umbulu.
(Phot. Hopwood.)

*A caravan of porters bringing provisions to the crater from the market township of Mbulu, 100 kilometres (60 miles) distant.*

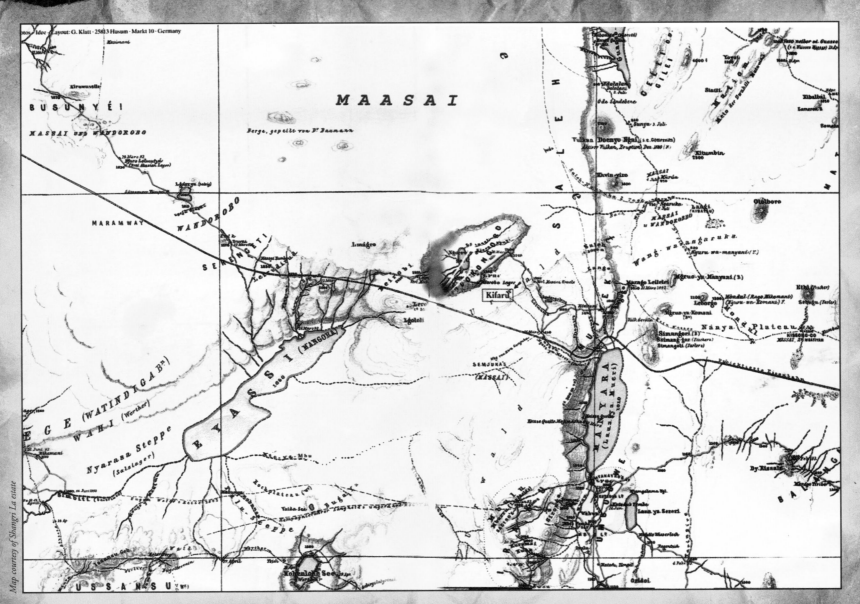

*An early German map of the area surrounding the Ngorongoro Crater, prepared by D O Baumann for the German Antislave Committee, 1894.*

*Soldiers of the German East African troops during the First World War. Under the leadership of General Paul von Lettow-Vorbeck, they were not defeated until they were called upon to capitulate to the British troops after Germany had lost the war in Europe.*

*Germans soldiers engaged in shooting practice, 1914.*

*Nasera rock, a weathered volcanic outcrop bearing witness to the turbulent geological history of the Ngorongoro.*

*An aerial view of Olduvai Gorge.*

# The Beginning

About six million years ago cataclysmic earthquakes and volcanic eruptions rocked most of the world, including northern Tanzania, to such an extent that they would dwarf into insignificance the biggest man-made explosions of today. It was the lava produced at this time that built up the volcanic range of the Crater Highlands, comprising Ngorongoro, Oldeani, Makarut, Lolmalasin, Olmoti, and Empakaai.

Some four million years later, in a massive movement of enormous tectonic plates, Africa was fractured down the centre from Turkey to Lake Nyasa, forming what has become known as the Great Rift Valley.

This further earth disturbance dramatically altered the six peaks of the Crater Highlands. Three, including Ngorongoro, collapsed inwards to form calderas, which are believed to be caused by the withdrawal of molten lava beneath a crater. Although commonly referred to as a crater, as it will be in this book, Ngorongoro is in fact the largest, unflooded, unbroken caldera in the world.

Situated in the Arusha Region of Tanzania, this vast depression averages 16 to 19 kilometres (10 to 12 miles) in diameter, and the rim varies in height from 2,280 metres (7,500 feet) to 2,440 metres (8,000 feet). The walls plunge steeply to the floor 600 metres (2,000 feet) below, which covers an area of some 264 square kilometres (102 square miles).

Although the most recent populations inhabiting the crater – the Nilo-Hamitic groups – arrived around 300 years ago, prehistoric remains were discovered in the renowned Olduvai Gorge, only 48 kilometres (30 miles) west of Ngorongoro, dating back some 2 to 2.5 million years. Further discoveries were made in nearby Laetoli dating back as many as 3 to 3.5 million years.

First to research this area was a German entomologist, Professor Kattwinkel, who accidentally discovered the gorge in 1911 whilst collecting butterflies. He found a large number of fossil bones on the erosion slopes, including the bones of the extinct three-toed horse *Hipparian*. This aroused great interest in Germany and an expedition under a famous German archaeologist, Professor Hans Reck, was sent to Olduvai two years later. Reck's expedition exceeded all expectations and he sent back to Berlin an astonishing variety of prehistoric animals. The 1,750 pieces he crated home included a mammoth, a hippo with eyes right at the top of its head, an outsized four-horned antelope, and another *Hipparian* similar to Kattwinkel's.

Dr Louis Leakey, a Kenyan archaeologist, saw the fossil collection in the Berlin Museum after the First World War and invited Professor Reck to join an expedition to the gorge in 1931. During this expedition Professor Reck, whose health no longer permitted strenuous fieldwork, formally handed over to Dr Leakey his permission for any further excavation in the gorge. This led to Dr Louis and his wife, Mary Leakey, discovering *Australopithecus boisei*, a human-like fossil dating back 1.75 million years, and subsequently *Homo habilis*, a true prehistoric 'humanoid humanus'.

After her husband's death in 1972, Mary Leakey continued her research at Olduvai and then, four years later at nearby Laetoli, made the exciting discovery of a fossil ancestor of man, including footprints, which dated back some 3.5 million years.

As the continual discovery of more recent fossils testifies, the close proximity of Olduvai and Laetoli to Ngorongoro Crater establishes that humans and animals have shared this area for millions of years.

Bridging the gap between the old fossils and the Maasai of today are the Neolithic gravesites dating back some 10,000 years. These were discovered at the north end of the crater before the First World War.

At the end of the 19th century two German brothers, Adolf and Fredrich Wilhelm Siedentopf, had started farming on the crater floor. One of their managers, a naturalist called Rothe, accidentally uncovered an ancient gravesite when collecting stone for farm buildings at the northern end of the crater. Rothe realized the importance of his find, and very carefully carried out a systematic excavation. In 1911 Rothe handed over a detailed report on his findings to Professor Reck, who stayed with the Siedentopfs before being introduced to Olduvai Gorge.

Rothe had uncovered what appeared to be an important grave, possibly that of a chief, together with 30 slaves or sacrifices. It contained a complete man's skeleton of unusual size in a position of natural sleep, with its head pointing to the south-west. Lying alongside him was a smaller skeleton and between the two were the remains of a small child. Reck surmised that the burial custom of that time may have been to kill and bury the wife of an important man, with her child, to accompany the man on his 'death safari'. Thirty more skulls were unearthed, all with their lower jawbones missing.

There were four small caves in the corner of the grave containing beautifully formed earthenware pots filled with black lentil-shaped seeds or food particles. Evidently the dead were buried with food and the pots it was served in.

There were no traces of metal in the grave, but obsidian splinters were found. As these splinters were the main working tool materials, Professor Reck stated that this would indicate a 'very high Stone Age culture'. The further discovery of rubbing stones for grinding flour, together with the remains of the above-mentioned pots and their contents, suggested an agricultural civilization rather than a nomadic one.

During the First World War Professor Reck returned to the site accompanied by a Dr Arning. They opened two more graves, and in these they found jewels made of quartz. Reck observed that 'The very fine work on the hard quartz showed an advanced technique.' They also found a three-pointed stone arrowhead and a necklace of 138 small round beads apparently made from the shells of snails or small animals. Two cowrie shells were also discovered, presumably originating from the coast.

*The sedimentary layers of Olduvai Gorge have yielded many exciting fossil discoveries.*

According to Reck, the grinding plates, quartz stones, and serpentine found in the graves must have been brought to the crater on long trips 'from ancient stone levels outside the volcanic district'.

Professor Reck writes that the Stone Age man of 10,000 BC used obsidian, although it was not detected in the country adjoining Ngorongoro. The substance had, however, been found in the lakes Naivasha and Nakuru area of Kenya, and seems to have been brought further south to Tanganyika.

The pastoral inhabitants of the crater during that period were known as the Stone Bowl People. They were named after the bowls they hammered out of volcanic rock; however, nothing is known of the tools used to work this hard, dark lava stone. Professor Reck states that there was a particularly high standard of handicraft, not only in the jewellery but also in the magnificently formed lava dishes found by him, Rothe, Siedentopf, and Arning.

Mary Leakey, together with an anthropologist, Major J Trevor, made further investigations of gravesites at Ngorongoro Crater in 1940, during the Second World War.

The Ngorongoro Conservation Area (NCA) is part of the Serengeti ecosystem where, at present, the miracle of the last great migration on earth takes place. There are more than two million animals on the move, mainly wildebeest and zebra. Those fortunate enough to witness this truly magnificent sight will, I am sure, never forget the experience! Preference for and selection of this region by animals has continued right through to the present day, and thus one finds the Ngorongoro Crater floor always full of activity.

International recognition of the importance to mankind of Ngorongoro Crater came in 1972 when it was declared a World Heritage Site of 'outstanding universal value'. It has also been referred to over recent years as 'the Eighth Wonder of the World' and 'the Cradle of Mankind'.

No less thrilling than the spectacular topography, the fascinating roots of civilization, and the incredible numbers and variety of game, is the story of how the crater came to be established as a game sanctuary.

Three administrations have been involved – German, British, and now the government of Tanzania. Many obstacles had to be overcome, including the resistance of individuals and of whole nations.

Two world wars have played their not inconsiderable part, and personal ambitions and intrigues have pitted themselves against the vision and forethought of a few far-sighted and public-spirited men. There can be no doubt, however, as to who has gained the final victory: the animals, and the tens of thousands of people who flock every year to see them. Nevertheless, the struggle has been long and hard, as the following chapters will show.

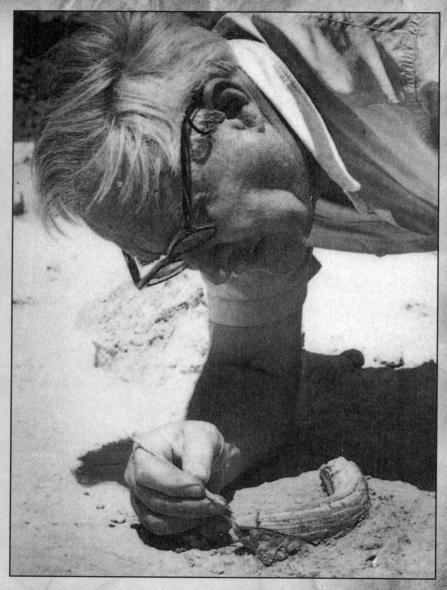

*Louis Leakey, working at Olduvai Gorge. He helped elevate African palaeontology to international status.*

*View across the floor of the Ngorongoro Crater.*

The magnificent vista presented by Empakaai Crater, north-east of Ngorongoro.

*The Gol Mountains, at the northern edge of the Ngorongoro Conservation Area.*

*The original Ngorongoro Crater lodge, as it was in the 1940s.*

*A pride of lions cools down at the edge of a muddy pool on the Ngorongoro Crater floor.*

*The regal profile of the most formidable member of the big cat family.*

*Marabou storks roosting in the broad crown of a tall acacia.*

*Maasai warriors with their distinctively patterned shields and other trappings of war.*

# The Maasai

It is impossible to understand the history or plan the future of Ngorongoro Crater without an insight into the way of life of the most recent inhabitants of the crater and its surrounding areas. Here we find one of the most colourful and interesting tribes in the African continent: the Maasai.

Their Nilo-Hamitic forefathers fought their way southwards through the African continent, following the River Nile, and herded their cattle freely across the Great Rift Valley of Africa. Their first encounter with Europeans was in the 1840s, when the Maasai attempts to resist their encroachment were defeated. For the past hundred years the Maasai's traditional way of life has been under increasing threat as the other tribes around them have developed but, remarkably, they have managed to hold on to many of their tribal customs, initiation rites, and superstitions. The Maasai have been one of the few African tribes to steadfastly resist progress and civilization, and their traditions have remained almost unchanged over the past four hundred years.

It is extremely difficult to pinpoint exactly when the Maasai arrived within the Ngorongoro Crater area. A 1958 memorandum on the Serengeti National Park, written by the British administration at the time, states: 'We do not know precisely how long Maasai have been in occupation of the country in the neighbourhood of the Ngorongoro Crater, but the period exceeds 150 years. The last but one *laigwenan* (elder or spokesman) of the Ngorongoro was born in the Lerai Forest, in the crater, during the first decade of the century, as was his great-grandfather.'

The legends of the *laibonok* (medicine men, singular *laibon*) make it likely that the Maasai were in Ngorongoro Crater long before the time stated in the memorandum. It is recorded by Hollis, who wrote the first book about the Maasai in 1904, that the chief laibon, Lenana, was ninth in succession. Allowing about thirty years for each generation, the first laibons, Aiser and Kileken (who, according to legend, were heaven-born boys found on the Ngong Hills in Kenya), would have existed around 1640. One can therefore presume that the history of the Maasai in East Africa dates back about four hundred years to the early 17th century.

Tanzania and Kenya's respective Maasailands merge at the northern end of Serengeti National Park. Any breakaway group of the tribe entering Tanzania in the 18th century would have been bound to discover the Ngorongoro Crater very quickly. With its lush grass and good permanent water, it is one of the finest pastoral areas in Africa.

During the years between 1860 and 1890, the Maasai were preoccupied with wars, raids against neighbouring tribes, and attacks on caravans led by early explorers. This phase is covered at length in the books written on early exploration.

A highly contagious febrile disease, rinderpest, then swept down from the Horn of Africa and was not halted until it had decimated the cattle and game throughout East,

*The chief laibon or spiritual leader of the Maasai in the Ngorongoro Highlands in 1967.*

*An elegantly coiffured Maasai moran.*

Central, and Southern Africa. Smallpox was simultaneously rampant in the land, and to complete what was to become known as 'the Triple Plague', locusts had swarmed over the countryside and ruined the grazing. Whole families of Maasai, together with their livestock, were wiped out at this time, and the tribe was scattered from the coast to Lake Victoria.

In the years that were to follow they returned to their old habitats and built up their family groups and herds again, whilst other tribes absorbed some of the remnants.

The extreme regard the Maasai have for the Ngorongoro area is no doubt attributable to the fact that, in their battle for survival, many of those who managed to weather the storms of misfortune were able to reach the crater during the plagues. This is why they so strongly resisted the proposal for reconstitution of the Serengeti National Park that suggested removal of the Maasai from the crater.

In order to follow this highly controversial and important issue, leading to the present development of the Ngorongoro Conservation Area Authority (NCAA), it is necessary to delve further into the background and traditions of this fascinating tribe.

The Maasai have a religion all of their own and their god is called Engai. They believe that Engai first created them, and then made and sent to Earth, specifically for them, cattle. Therefore, it is their belief that ALL cattle, ipso facto, belong to the Maasai tribe. This belief has resulted in constant warfare over the centuries as the Maasai have attempted to take, from other tribes, the livestock they believe belongs to them. During the 18 years I farmed in Oldeani, a district next to the crater, the Maasai would often emerge from the forest reserve and attack the Wambulu tribe in order to rustle their cattle. These encounters often resulted in many deaths on both sides.

European missionaries in Africa very seldom succeed in convincing the tribe members that they should convert to Christianity, and even when converted they interpret the faith in light of their own traditions. Recently Maasai conversion shot up when, at a preaching rally, a pertinent question was asked and then answered 'correctly'. A member of the congregation asked: 'We know God and his prophet Aiser, but who is Jesus?' The churchman's reply was: 'Due to the hearts of mankind God had to send another prophet after Aiser. His name was Jesus.' This appeared to be a satisfactory explanation.

The Maasai have two loves in life – cattle and fighting. Cattle are the centre of Maasai life and they consider nothing else of equal value. They provide food in the form of milk, blood, and meat; the skins are used for some items of their clothing; the dung is used for sealing their houses; and the live animals provide the negotiated bridal price before marriage. Over the years the herd is in turn increased by the additions made by the bridal price for girl children. Much trouble is taken to mark the herd with a personalized brand and ear slits that give a positive identification of the clan, family, and individual owner.

Unlike practically all other African tribes, the Maasai do not normally touch game meat – their principal food is milk. One of their traditions is to occasionally mix cow's blood with the milk. They draw the blood by tying a leather ligature around the neck of the beast and a vein is pierced with an arrow – according to veterinary officers this process is quite painless. The blood is then collected in gourds and is predominantly drunk by the *moran* (warriors) either neat or, as previously mentioned, mixed with milk.

The elders, women, and children mainly eat maize, bananas, beans, and other cereals. They only eat meat when the livestock have died naturally, a bullock or sheep has been slaughtered for a ceremony, or when the wife is nursing a child. The time of the Triple Plague in the 1890s was an exception. This accounts for the fact that the game in Tanzanian and Kenyan national parks and reserves, where the Maasai prevail, is more prolific than anywhere else in Africa. Their discipline and continual preparedness for war has kept other game-eating tribes out of Maasailand.

The tribe is split into subtribes, clans, and family groups, and the males are separated into five age groups: child, junior warrior, senior warrior, junior elder, and senior elder. This age-group system forms the basis of the Maasai social organization. All young men, after being circumcised in their teens, belong to an age set which is given a name as might be that of a regiment. After seven years as junior warriors, a promotion ceremony elevates all the members of the group to the rank of senior warriors. A further seven years later there is a standing-down ceremony by which junior elderhood is attained. During all this time further youths have been circumcised and promoted to fill the ranks of the warrior group, and so the cycle repeats itself. The warriors are known as *moran*, and the leader or spokesman of the section is known as the *laigwenan*.

Before becoming a moran, the boy child's duty is to herd his father's cattle. Should a lion or leopard attack the cattle the youth is expected to defend the cattle to the best of his ability before running home to report the incident. It is then that the moran come into their own – they must hunt down and attack the predator. The spearing of a lion by a particular age group of moran is the most spectacular and thrilling fulfilment of warriorhood. Generally, the lion, which takes the principal but unwished-for role in the drama, is the one which has killed or mauled livestock. It is tracked down, surrounded by the moran, and provoked to charge. The warrior finding himself in the direct line of the lion's escape takes the full brunt of the charge on his shield and spear before his comrades come to his assistance. Together they then hack the lion to pieces with their spears and *simis* (short, twin-bladed swords).

After circumcision and initiation into his warrior clan, the Maasai youth leaves his father's *boma* (small village), and goes to a separate *manyatta*. This is a warrior's village where only the moran, their mothers, and their uncircumcised girlfriends live. It is interesting to note that the moran have access to all unmarried Maasai girls before they (the moran) are married or become elders. Whilst living at the manyatta they normally do not marry.

Most of their time is spent participating in various war ceremonies, keeping themselves fit and ready to fight. This tradition, which has continued through the centuries, has always ensured a large number of warriors trained and ready for war – somewhat similar in principle to the national service of today in many countries.

The warriors seldom go more than six months without disappearing into the bush for their meat-eating ceremony, called *ol-pul*. They generally turn the safari into a forced march, which, together with other self-imposed hardships, forms part of the toughening-up process. The bullock they have taken with them to a hide situated some distance from their manyatta is killed and eaten to the last piece of flesh.

The moran may leave the manyatta in order to assist their families, during which time their duties would include such chores as drawing water from the wells for the cattle, cutting thorn trees for the boma stockade, escorting home night-moving cattle, and searching for lost livestock.

A typical Maasai warrior dressed in his full regalia is a truly magnificent sight. He stands 1.8 metres (6 feet) tall, and his slim, athletic body is clothed in the conventional ochre-stained *amerikani* cloth. His hairstyle is very elaborate and is covered in sheep or bovine fat mixed with ochre. The style will be in one of three different forms – one or more pigtails formed into a plait around a stick; a ridged helmet heavily plastered with fat or oil; or long and loosely plaited.

The elaborate headdress that frames his face is made from lion mane or ostrich feathers. The warrior wearing a lion mane headdress may do so if he has killed the animal himself.

Around his waist he wears a leather belt with a simi in a red leather scabbard, and one or more wooden knobkerries made from an iron-hard tree root. He carries a 2-metre (7-foot) spear, almost a metre (3 feet) of which is sharpened blade of pliable steel, and a shield which is multicoloured. Markings on the shield indicate the age group he belongs to, and his clan and subdistrict. In isolated cases there might be an insignia such as a star showing that the individual has displayed exceptional bravery on a certain occasion. Generally the shield is painted in red obtained from red ochre, white from ash or lime deposits, and black from charcoal. The blue and pink often seen today is from dye purchased at stores.

When his warrior days are over the moran, and his companions of the same age group, will graduate to the elder group in a ceremony known as *ol-ngesher*. At this stage all signs of warriorhood are abandoned and his pigtails are cut off. Then, if not already married, he finds a wife at the earliest opportunity and marries her. The senior member of the age group is selected as *ol-oosurutia*, or head of that generation. He has no special duties but is treated with great respect.

Those moran who are already married, together with those who have married after becoming elders, may leave their family bomas and establish their own. They will generally break away with three or four members of the same age group, taking with them their share of their fathers' cattle. The boma then comprises a ring of huts encircled by a thorn stockade housing several groups of married couples and their families. Each family has its own entrance.

An elder may have as many wives as he can afford, paying the bridal price to the fathers-in-law. The customary bridal price is three heifers and one bull, but often it is a matter of prestige to give more. I knew a very wealthy Maasai who lived in the Serengeti in the early 1950s who owned 9,000 cattle and 40 wives! A poor man marrying the daughter of a rich man may be given cattle as well as a wife by the father-in-law, without paying the full bridal price. Each new arrival in the matrimonial field is given a number of cattle by her husband, normally eight cows and one bull, and these are hers to hold in trust for her children. The problem of the barren wife is solved by one of the wives with one or more children – she exchanges one of her children for a cow and a calf.

The hospitality an elder may receive when visiting and spending the night at the boma of one of his own age group would appear to be almost overwhelming! His host allocates one of the wives' huts and he may share her bed for the night at her discretion. Alternatively, she may leave the master bed to the guest and move to the children's bed.

The Maasai ladies are as vain as their European counterparts and wear attractive ornaments, some of which have particular significance. They wear large, wide, circular necklaces that are made of row upon row of beaded designs in various colours. Their arms and legs have copper wire wound around them. The married woman wears special earrings and anklet bangles, and she will never remove these during her husband's lifetime. Young girls wear beads, small pieces of iron, wire bracelets, and anklets made of iron. Personal bejewelling is not only enjoyed by the women; the men also decorate themselves. Warriors and elders also wear adornments in the form of earrings and chain bracelets, and young males put wooden blocks in their ear lobes, gradually increasing the size until the opening can hold a large snuffbox!

Finally, we come to the most important members of the tribe in their social structure, the *laibonok*. The Maasai are split into clans and the spiritual leaders within these clans are the laibonok or medicine men.

*A Maasai moran warrior armed with a long-bladed spear.*

Beaded earrings and necklaces of Maasai woman.

Maasai girl with newborn kid.

*Heavy beaded earrings have gradually elongated the earlobes of this Maasai man.*

*A young Maasai herdsman at Ngorongoro typifies the continuing dedication of the Maasai to their traditional pastoral existence.*

There are three different types of laibonok. The first, the 'general practitioner', will perform for suitable remuneration such services as the cure of sickness, removing barrenness, and preventing wives from running away from their husbands. The second, the 'private practitioner', is a man who has acquired such a reputation that a deputation on behalf of a group of Maasai consults him. He then provides charms and lays down a ceremonial to be utilized to the advantage of the whole group. His services are considered necessary for procuring success in war, adequate rainfall, or immunity from diseases (both human and bovine). The third and most important laibon is invited to superintend and bless ceremonies affecting the whole district group, such as circumcision, promoting and standing down warrior age groups, and so on.

Upon the death of a Maasai, the hyena is the official undertaker of the body. The body is removed from the boma and placed on the ground. Should it be left untouched by the hyenas and vultures after two or three days, the bones of a bullock are left with the corpse in order to attract them to carry the body away.

An entirely different ritual is followed for the laibonok and very rich cattle owners, for whom a grave may be dug. The body is anointed with oil, put in an oxhide, and taken to the grave, which is usually in a shady spot within the boma. Once the body has been buried the grave is covered with stones, and Maasai passing the spot throw a stone into the pile 'for evermore'.

The respect the Maasai have for the more outstanding members of their tribe made it very understandable that they should be horrified at the suggestion in the memorandum on the Serengeti National Park that they should not be allowed to visit their graves in the Lerai Forest on the crater floor. Any restrictions on visits to the Lerai would affect not only the Maasai but also the Datoga, now living in the Lake Eyasi area. Tradition has it that some of the enormous fig trees in the forest were planted around the grave of a famous Datoga leader killed in battle with the Maasai towards the middle of the 19th century. The Maasai conquered the Datoga and forced them out of the crater, which they had previously occupied. Present day Datoga still make pilgrimages to the gravesite and leave offerings there. Another example of the importance of this location to the Maasai occurs during a drought period, when the women fasten grass to their clothes and offer prayers to their god, Engai, soliciting rain.

It has been estimated that there are about 250,000 traditionally recognizable Maasai living on the plains of the Tanzanian and Kenyan Maasailands, and that they have a total of at least two million cattle and as many goats and sheep. Although a large proportion of their habitat includes desert-like country used only for grazing after the rains, a considerable amount of the 210,000 square kilometres (80,000 square miles) comprising the Maasailands is first-class land with potential for agricultural development. If the Maasai do not change their traditional pastoralist life to one of mixed farming, thus utilizing their land better, they will undoubtedly find it progressively more difficult to retain the vast areas they possess. At present, however, with a total population of 30 million inhabiting a territory of 950,000 square kilometres (365,000 square miles), there is no land shortage in Tanzania, and there is plenty of available land awaiting development.

It is, however, a different story in Kenya, despite the transfer of ownership, after independence, of hundreds of thousands of acres from European to African hands. Kenya also has a high birth rate, estimated at over five children per family. As the population increases in both territories there will be more pressure from other agriculturist tribes to move into Maasailand.

It is doubtful if the governments in either Kenya or Tanzania will be able to resist this pressure – if, indeed, they wished to – considering the present rate of development and the great economic potential for agricultural planning in many parts of Maasailand.

Fortunately, at the time of the reconstruction of the Serengeti National Park in 1959, the British government carried out some far-sighted planning of the crater. Since then it has been utilized as the pivot for a comprehensive development project administered by the NCAA. Although not including agriculture, this development is advantageous to the Maasai and their livestock, to the game in the area, and to the country of Tanzania, as I will explain in a further chapter.

If this pilot project continues successfully and the necessary money and technical know-how are available for similar schemes in other parts of Maasailand, the Maasai stand a chance of survival. This would inevitably involve changing their current way of life.

Elliot and Hollis wrote over 90 years ago: 'The only hope is that under intelligent guidance they may gradually settle down and adopt a certain measure of civilization. Any plan of leaving them to themselves with their old military and social organization seems fraught with grave danger for the prosperity of the tribe, as well as for public peace.' This is proving to be as relevant today as it was then, with most Maasai still steadfastly refusing to accept change.

The Tanzanian government is indeed providing intelligent guidance and is extremely sympathetic to the Maasai problem. It is therefore possible that a compromise solution will be found by implanting a degree of civilization whilst, at the same time, making it possible for this unique tribe to retain the traditions, ceremonies, and superstitions which have remained virtually unchanged throughout the centuries.

The Maasai the tourists see at the Ngorongoro Crater today are, currently, unchanged and unspoilt, but their future is precarious.

A herd of zebra wanders between a Maasai herdsman and a stockaded settlement.

*Enough for all? Wildebeest file past a herd of Maasai cattle, the wild and the domesticated sharing their environment.*

*Maasai family outside their mud and dung home. Strong codes of discipline and stoicism enable the Maasai to live cheerfully in their harsh environment.*

*A Maasai moran proudly displays his hairstyle.*

*Young Maasai women, recovering from clitoridectomy, proclaim their new status by wearing traditional beaded headbands around their cropped hair. Now they will learn the rights and duties of womanhood and become eligible to marry.*

*Maasai herdsmen escort their cattle towards the alkaline waters of Lake Magadi. Although they are no longer allowed to live inside the crater, they still have watering and grazing rights.*

*View across the floor of the Ngorongoro crater.*

# Dr Oscar Baumann

It is difficult for today's traveller to imagine the tremendous physical effort and hazards of the African foot safaris undertaken by the first explorers during the 19th century. Such an explorer was the German Dr Oscar Baumann, who became, on 18 March 1892, the first white man to see the Ngorongoro Crater.

Probably the best detailed record of a safari of this type is that found in Joseph Thomson's book *Through Maasailand*. Thomson's trip was made nine years earlier than Baumann's, almost to the day, and was a Royal Geographical Society expedition which reached only the eastern fringe of northern Maasailand, near Mount Kilimanjaro, some 275 kilometres (170 miles) south-east of the Ngorongoro. There they had to turn back owing to the warlike behaviour of the Maasai, who had attacked a caravan led by another explorer, Dr Fischer, shortly before.

Both Thomson and Baumann penetrated Maasailand, but Baumann travelled further west into the heart of Maasailand, approaching Lake Victoria, which was why he came across the Ngorongoro Crater.

The personnel, equipment, and organization of Thomson's foot portage safari would have been very similar to that of Baumann's. It is interesting to read a description of Thomson's caravan when he left the coast to start his trip, as it gives us an idea of the sheer size of such an expedition and what it entailed. His colourful portrayal of the characteristics and responsibilities of those accompanying him enables us to visualize the individuals hired to undertake this adventure. His detailed comments on their appearance also show that men of different tribes were employed for various specific tasks. He wrote:

'Taking my men according to rank there naturally steps forth my safari assistant, James Martin, familiarly known as Martin. Comparatively short of limb, though stout of body, he has the somewhat ungraceful walk of the sailor. Dark eyes and hair and swarthy complexion at once indicate that he comes of a Mediterranean race.

'Next appears Muhinna, on whose honesty I depend for any success in my attempt to penetrate Maasai territory. A cunning, unprepossessing expression does not speak well for him, but at present I have no fault to find with him.

'Following Muhinna appear, in succession, Muinya Sera, short and well up in years; Makatubu, tall, well-made and muscular; Kacheche, "the Detective", rather below the average in size, characterized by a sly expression, as of one who has some "ways that are dark, and tricks that are vain".

'In the wake of these worthies comes Brahim ("the Bullock"), as faithful as a bulldog, and almost as unprepossessing in appearance.

'The rear of the headmen is brought up by Mzee (Swahili: "the Old Man"), Nauledi, the quiet and steady, with a cast of features and a wealth of beard that tell of Arab blood in his veins.

'After the leaders appear Bedue ("the Wanderer"), a perfect giant, bold and strong, but woefully lazy. He acts as the captain of those men who follow, viz., ten *askari* (soldiers or guards). These askari are the best men picked for the caravan, and their duties are to act as guards, police, hunters, and general assistants of the headmen.

'I had none with me on my first expedition, but it would have been impossible to do without them on this occasion, so incessant was the watchfulness required to prevent desertion, and to guard the camp, not to speak of the unusual amount of work required on arriving in camp, which hardly came under the duties of the porters. Songoro, my "boy", comes next to him in point of rank, and my pen fails me to describe his admirable qualities. He was simply perfection as an upcountry servant.

'Along with these, however, must be mentioned my cook – a Nassick boy named Mark Wellington, well intentioned and honest, but so atrociously slow and stupid that he spoiled more of my food than I care to think of now.

'Finally, following the askaris, come the rank and file, the porters – an indescribable lot! Therefore let me pass them on with the remark that there were 122 in all, and that they were loaded as follows: 29 carrying beads; 34, iron, brass, and copper wire; 14, cloth; 15, personal stores; 9, clothes, boots, books, etc.; 5, ammunition; 6, scientific instruments, photographic apparatus, etc.; 10, tents and tent furniture, cooking gear, etc. If you add two boys, one gun bearer and one donkey-boy, you have the list of my caravan complete.

'Such then were the component elements of the Royal Geographical Society's expedition to one of the most dangerous, unexplored regions of Africa, when on the fifteenth of March, 1883, it stood in the sweltering midday heat, in the centre of the mission settlement, awaiting the word to start.'

Let us now join Baumann on his approach to the Ngorongoro as he climbs the Great Rift wall nine years later on 13 March 1892. At this stage he finds himself about 55 kilometres (35 miles) from the Ngorongoro Crater. The point at which Baumann climbed is considerably to the north of the Great Rift wall, and the Manyara Hotel, but the description tallies exactly with what the traveller sees today from the observation point at the top of the scarp. He wrote:

'March 13 was taken up with an exhausting climb to the plateau. A narrow Maasai cattle track led along a slope that had an outcrop of enormous basalt boulders and up which men could advance quite well, but donkeys and cattle only with difficulty. When, after a strenuous ascent, we arrived at the magnificent plateau, it was almost evening.

'There on the top a wonderful view of the shimmering Lake Manyara compensated us for our efforts. From this point the lake is visible for the whole of its extent, showing the steep western banks and Ufiomi Mountain to the south. With its discovery one of the main missions of the Maasai expedition was fulfilled.

*Dr Oscar Baumann, the first white man to see the Ngorongoro Crater, 18 March 1892.*

'Cool, clean air refreshed us, and at this height clear streams rushed down between slopes covered with fine grass. A dark, forested mountain range appeared in the north.'

It is possible that the path climbed by Baumann was the same one used 10 years afterwards by the Siedentopf brothers, with wagons, when they settled in the crater. This path is near an ancient stone village site at Ngaruka, at the foot of the scarp.

'Next morning we set out for a short march only and camped at Llmoro stream, where we spent one complete day repacking our loads.' Llmoro stream appears on Obst's German map, and also on the first British map as Olmoro. It is the northernmost of the streams which, rising in the highland reserve, drain into Lake Manyara, so therefore Baumann's camp lay well to the north of the present motor road.

Wambugwe warriors had attacked the caravan just before and there was a fierce skirmish before the attackers withdrew. 'The loss of men since Mbugwe had now become noticeable, also our pack animals had suffered from the bites of the *ndorobo* (tsetse) fly. This insect is to be found near streams and is dangerous for donkeys, as they bite the donkey's anus, which causes swelling and leads to the animal's death.'

The tsetse fly is still prevalent below the Rift, as visitors to the Manyara National Park will have observed. It was between the lakeshore and the Rift, an area now included in the park, that Baumann travelled and where, doubtless, the donkeys became infected with trypanosomiasis. This is indeed a disease fatal to donkeys; it does not, however, manifest the symptoms recorded.

'We urgently required new herdsmen for our cattle herd and our loads were not substantially reduced. To reduce the number of loads, the weight of some bundles containing clothes was increased and various pieces of clothing were distributed to the porters, as an advance for their services. Even then, too many loads remained, and I came to the conclusion that I would have to dispose of some loads since, by delaying our safari, the whole success of the safari might be endangered. We therefore proceeded to dig a pit and put in glass beads, brass wire, various music boxes and other junk, which might be useful when one travels in Africa but, on the other hand, one might just as well be without it. We filled in the pit and lit a fire over it, following Kiburandgop's advice, as he maintained that the ashes would mark the place, even after many years.

'We had now recovered our former mobility, and it only remained to replace the five askaris from the ranks of our porters. I had earmarked some people for such a situation long ago. Their extraordinary efficiency had drawn my attention to them.

'One man, by the name of Bakari Juma, deserves a particular mention. He was a real Digo and knew no Swahili. He was a thickset fellow possessed of extraordinary strength. His large, jet-black head was set between broad shoulders, almost without a neck. The face bore a striking resemblance to that of a hippopotamus. Sharp, enterprising eyes looked out from this face, which was not improved by smallpox. But, in spite of this, one immediately took a liking to him. He proved himself later to be an excellent askari. Whenever there was an attack, or other dangerous event, Juma went out in front of everybody. He was also an untiring worker. Once, when circumstances demanded it, he carried two loads on his head, and a sick fellow askari on his back, for many hours.

'The newly appointed askaris were issued with their uniform and, on March 16, the journey was continued over the plateau. The absence of a guide was very hampering, as everything was completely strange to Ndaikai, and also Kiburandgop could no longer remember the route. As long as the march lay over open, grassed hilltops, progress was comparatively easy, but as we had to pass through a forest we definitely required a guide.

'The presence of two Maasai Ilmurran, who appeared suddenly near the Murera stream, was therefore very opportune. They told us that they had been attracted by the smell of our cattle. Needless to say we did not want to lose such welcome guests. One of the guests was the leader (laigwenan) of the young people of Mutyek. He was a strikingly good-looking fellow, having delicate, attractive features and a slim, perfectly proportioned body. He told us that his people were at present engaged in a fight against the Wambugwe, and asked whether we had met them. We thought immediately of the incident at Lake Manyara, and declared that we had, in fact, made a "flying acquaintance" with these gentlemen. It impressed the laigwenan tremendously that we had beaten the Wambugwe, and had taken a lot of their cattle, as the Maasai had never managed to accomplish this. From then onwards he became a very enthusiastic friend, and even proposed a partnership for cattle pilfering! He naturally had never seen a white man before. Even now he had no idea that I was a representative of another race, but thought I was a different type of coastal Negro.'

The Wambugwe being referred to are a Bantu tribe living to this day to the south of Lake Manyara. As intrepid spearmen, they were one of the few Bantu tribes to stand up against the Maasai.

'On the morning of March 17th the warriors, marching vigorously ahead, had found a red cattle track which climbed through beautiful, grass-covered slopes and brought us into thick, tropical forest. Entangled, herbaceous vegetation and numerous nettles covered the ground. Thick, short trees stood here and there, their branches covered with moss and lichen on the windward side, and entwined with numerous creepers. We camped in the forest near a murmuring stream over which butterflies fluttered. In the evening thick mist descended and it became quite cold.'

According to the description of this day's march, they had proceeded through the Nailangalanga series of glades. People have claimed to have detected evidence of severe

*One of the starveling Maasai encountered by Oscar Baumann on his visit to the crater in 1892.*

forest destruction over recent years; however, it is significant that Baumann speaks of 'open grassland with occasional scattered groves' rather than forest broken by occasional glades.

Then, after a steady climb, came the great moment when Baumann made history as the first recorded white man to see the Ngorongoro Crater, spread out below like a map. Judging by his comments he did not seem to be as awestruck as most visitors are when they first set eyes on the spectacular view of the crater from the same spot, now marked by a board, on the east rim road.

'On March 18th we pushed on through the mountain forest over a good cattle track, flanked on either side by thick walls of vegetation. Starting at 9 a.m. we passed through open grassland with marshy rills and scattered, charming groves. At noon we suddenly found ourselves on the rim of a sheer cliff and looked down into the bowl of the Ngorongoro, the remains of an old crater.

'The crater floor was grassland, alive with game; there was a small lake on the western side. We went down the steep slope and started to pitch our tents at the foot of the precipice. At nightfall several Maasai warriors were seen prowling around camp, probably with the intention of stealing cattle. The number of sentries was accordingly doubled and the rest of the night was quiet.

'March 19th. Early, at dawn, we marched over a gently undulating plain. The soil was black humus covered with good grass and, in places, with volcanic rubble.

'We were escorted in the morning mist by a great number of Maasai warriors, strongly built, picturesque fellows with colourful shields and bright, broad-pointed spears.' Interestingly, the Maasai no longer use broad-bladed spears. Possibly this is due to the importation of iron bars since the turn of the century, or even wire, which enabled the smiths to beat out longer blades from the indigenously smelted iron than they could formerly.

'We made our camp near a small wood in the shade of a giant tree. The air is always cool and fresh on the mountain range, doubly appreciable at noon when sunrays were penetrating the damp, morning mist. There was nothing to remind one of the tropics but swarms of flies, which often affect the Maasai with a form of trachoma. For a hunter our camp would have been paradise. Close to the small wood were numerous guineafowl, of which I shot a few for breakfast. Hippopotami snorted in a pool and terrific herds of game were roaming in the wide plains; they were hardly shy at all, although they had been hunted by the Wanderobo and recently also by the Maasai. The latter hunted game mainly by using their spears. They follow the wildebeest, which do not run very fast, and kill them with their spears. They approach the sleeping or grazing rhino in a snakelike fashion and spear it at close range.'

*Wildebeest, hunted by the Maasai at the time of Baumann's visit.*

*A hyena, on the lookout for an opportunistic meal, disturbs a group of wildebeest.*

It is of interest that Baumann describes Wanderobo being present in the crater. The word 'Wanderobo' is the Swahili version of the Maasai *Ol-Toroboni*, plural *Il-Toroboo*, meaning hunting folk. Included in this general term are the click-speaking hunters of the Ruiru valley and the Maasai-speaking Dorobo who, together with the metalworking smiths, form a low caste among the Maasai, and who doubtless migrated with them from the north. It is most probably to the last-named category that the Wanderobo met by Baumann belong.

'We rested for a day at the Ngorongoro and I took advantage of the opportunity to look at some of the Maasai kraals. In the inner courtyard, which was surrounded by low, hide-covered, tentlike huts, the Ilmurran greeted me with "Sowai". In front of the huts squatted old men whose features were sharply defined, while *inditos* (girls), decked out with iron ornaments and glass beads, peeped out from huts, with shining black eyes.'

Baumann's following account of the starving Maasai gives us an insight into how the people must have suffered during the Triple Plague.

'In the meantime a crowd of tattered scarecrows, now typical of Maasai country, gathered outside the thorn fence of our camp. There were women reduced to walking skeletons, out of whose sunken eyes peered the madness of hunger; children resembling deformed frogs rather than human beings; warriors who could hardly crawl on all fours; and moronic, emaciated greybeards.

'These people ate everything available; dead donkeys were a delicacy with them – but they also devoured the shins, bones, and even the horns of the cattle. I gave these unfortunate people as much food as I could, and the good-natured porters shared their rations with them; but their hunger was unappeasable, and they came in even greater numbers. They were refugees from the Serengeti, where starvation had depopulated whole districts.

'We were daily confronted by this misery and could do almost nothing to help. Parents offered their children in exchange for a piece of meat! When we refused to barter they artfully hid their children in the camp and escaped. Soon our camp was swarming with Maasai children and it was touching to see how the porters cared for the little urchins. I employed some of the stronger men and women as cowherds and thus saved a number from death by starvation.'

Baumann's friendly reception by the Maasai is typical of what the visitor may expect today. This tribe is completely satisfied with its own way of life and, in consequence, respects others who have different standards and values.

'On March 21st we penetrated into the Ngorongoro Crater, passing a Wanderobo camp which was surrounded and littered with game refuse, over which ravens, vultures, and marabou storks were fighting. We halted in a pleasant acacia forest near the lake. The plain was populated by numerous rhino, one of which I shot.'

The 'pleasant acacia forest near the lake' is doubtless Lerai, where elephant, waterbuck, baboon, and other forest-loving species still abound.

'In the afternoon Mzimba went hunting for the first time in his life, and shot a rhino. Several others in my expedition shot these beasts, as hunting them is not nearly so difficult and dangerous as it is claimed by the professional Nimrods. The rhino is not very shy and, if the wind is favourable, one can easily approach to within thirty paces without disturbing them. To hit a rhino at thirty paces you do not have to be a spectacular shot and, if the bullet hits the chest or, with a smaller calibre gun, the head, the animal usually collapses without further ado. If wounded anywhere else it either runs away at such speed that there is little chance of catching it, or it attacks the hunter.

'The moment is usually one described with horror by the Nimrods. The companions flee and only the hunter bravely faces the "charging colossus". This sounds terribly dangerous but the charging colossus is nearly blind and one step aside is sufficient to make it miss and it charges past. When it stops and looks around for its enemy the hunter has plenty of time to kill it with another bullet at close range.'

It is perhaps a pity that Baumann passed through the crater in March, for it has been noticed that the rhino population seems to reach its peak during that month, and according to his narration, it is sad to note that so many rhino were shot during his safari. Further to the east Count Teleki's expedition in 1886, travelling from Kilimanjaro to Lake Rudolph, disposed of 99 rhino. A further 66 rhino were killed in four months by a group of Indian Army officers, Captain Willoughby and two others, whilst hunting around the eastern slopes of Kilimanjaro. Detailed study of their accounts reveals what havoc some of the early explorers caused among game, particularly elephant and rhino.

'In the evening Wanderobo arrived in our camp and told us, in confidence, that some Maasai from a neighbouring kraal intended to attack us. I doubted very much that someone would dare to attack us, nevertheless I ordered the thorn fence to be built particularly carefully, and increased the sentries during the night. I had hardly returned to my tent when I heard the crack of a rifle. Everyone ran to the fence and I lit a magnesium flare, specifically brought for that purpose. We captured two stark-naked Maasai warriors who had tried to get into the cattle enclosure. We feared that we might be attacked but there were no further incidents of this kind, except that our sentries once fired in the dark on some approaching figures.

*Relaxing hippos enjoy the 'pleasant acacia forest near the lake' mentioned by Baumann during his exploration of the crater.*

'Next morning we were horrified to see two dead starvelings outside the fence. Beside them stood a thin, old man with untidy white hair, heaping furious curses on our heads. "You wallow in milk and meat", he cried, "and shoot at us who are dying of hunger. Curses on you."

'I arranged for some meat to be given to the poor old man, which he swallowed raw, only to start cursing us again. Even after we had moved off the cries of the pitiable old fellow followed us for some distance.'

The unfortunate incident of the shot Maasai typifies the period during which Baumann travelled. East Africa was opened up by armed caravans, originally Arab and Swahili, and the explorers took over the organization they found in the country.

The Maasai had a tremendous reputation among the Swahili porters and caravan leaders, so it is quite understandable that they should try to get in the first shot even though the Ngorongoro Maasai were in such pitiful condition at this time.

'We climbed the steep western slope of the crater bowl along a good cattle track and reached the Nairobi plateau, which is 2,400 metres (approx. 7,500 feet) above sea level.'

With this entry in his diary we leave Dr Baumann's caravan as it continued westwards from the Ngorongoro Crater.

*Hippo adult and youngster.*

*A moran (junior warrior) of the Maasai.*

*Bäumann encountered many rhino on the floor of the crater.*

*An acacia tree silhouetted in the red glow of sunset.*

*Adolf Siedentopf (second right) seated next to his wife, Paula. Also pictured are Paula's companion, Eva, and Adolf's brother Fredrich Wilhelm (centre back).*

# Adolf Siedentopf

## 'The feared, unapproachable King of the Ngorongoro'

Shortly after Baumann's pioneering safari, Germany declared the territory a colony and named it Deutsche Ost Afrika (German East Africa). After the First World War the newly formed League of Nations made the territory a mandate of Britain, who administered it as Tanganyika until its independence in 1961. Zanzibar joined Tanganyika in 1964 and the union was called Tanzania.

The crater was occupied or visited by several outstanding pioneers and hunters from the end of the 19th century right up to comparatively recent times.

Towering head and shoulders over all of them, in all respects – particularly physically, being 1.93 metres (6 feet 4 inches) in height and of phenomenally powerful physique – was the German, Adolf Siedentopf: explorer, prospector, farmer, chemist, hunter, and naturalist. He must have been a fascinating character, as prior to the First World War visitors to the crater, writing about their travels, devoted a large part of their memoirs to this legendary man.

It is well worthwhile studying Adolf's background in order to visualize and understand the type of man he was, and why he decided to choose this remote, game-filled corner of Tanzania to pioneer a farming operation.

He was born in Germany in 1872 at Farm Teichof, near Jerxheim in the Braunschweig district, as the eldest son of a German farmer, Fredrich Wilhelm Siedentopf. A quiet, reserved, husky youngster, his childhood ambition was to pioneer in Africa. Directly he left school he started studying chemistry and then Kiswahili, the lingua franca of East Africa, at the Oriental Languages Institute in Berlin. These efforts were to prepare him for Africa. When his father died in 1898 Adolf, as the eldest of three sons, inherited the farm. His father no doubt hoped that he would give up his 'hare-brained scheme' of emigrating to Africa, and that he would settle at Farm Teichof and continue the family tradition.

I corresponded with his wife's niece, Ursula Oetker, in the early 1960s, and she wrote: 'He wanted, however, a "free" life, and farming in Germany was far too narrow a horizon for him.'

Adolf was determined to fulfil his ambition of adventuring overseas, and, in 1898, after passing the farm over to one of his brothers, he travelled by ship to Germany's new colony, disembarking at the port of Tanga. There he worked for a short period at a biological institute, but most certainly would have been frustrated with life, spending much time daydreaming and preparing for safaris that would lead him to the enormous tracts of unexplored land awaiting him upcountry.

After a short spell exploring and prospecting, Adolf wrote to his brother Fredrich in 1902 suggesting that he should leave Germany and join him in a farming venture at the Ngorongoro. At the time he was cattle trading in Maasailand and had, the previous year,

succeeded in obtaining permission from the government to arm six cattle askaris with shotguns in order to combat Maasai rustlers. By 1904 Adolf and Fredrich had started farming on the crater floor together.

According to Hans Reck, the Siedentopf brothers spent the next four years hunting wildebeest and trading their tails (for use as fly whisks) with the Maasai in exchange for cattle.

Gert Fourie, a famous South African hunter, visited the crater in 1908 for a few days and stayed with the brothers. Gert Fourie's son, also named Gert, was a neighbouring farmer of mine in Karatu, and he showed me his father's diary containing details of this visit and a wealth of other fascinating information. He wrote that Adolf told him they had trekked some 2,000 head of cattle from Mwanza, on Lake Victoria, to the crater. Unfortunately there is no detailed record of this, what must have been an epic safari.

One can only imagine the hardships and adventures undergone by the brothers and their askaris, trekking an enormous herd of cattle some 320 kilometres (200 miles) right through the heart of Maasailand. A safari of this nature, even today, would be no mean undertaking. There are only a few, widely spaced permanent water points, so the safari must have been made during or directly after the rains, when the waterholes are full, there is fresh grass, and the normal game migration is in full flood.

Although several explorers had crossed the Serengeti and north Maasailand by that time, and the Germans had already established a flourishing cotton-growing development at Mwanza, most of Maasailand was still unexplored. The majority of Maasai had never met a white man, but in view of their 'attachment' to cattle and fighting, they would certainly have repeatedly attacked the safari and attempted to kill the white interlopers in order to steal their livestock.

The Serengeti has always been justifiably famous for its lion population, particularly during the migration, when a thousand lions prey on over two million animals. Lions frequently enjoy cattle as a change of diet and would also have been a continual threat.

So here we have the picture of the intrepid pioneers, accompanied by a handful of askaris, successfully completing a tedious, tough, 200-mile trek, with 2,000 cattle, and under conditions that would have astonished the famed Wild West cowboy cattle drovers of America!

Why Adolf decided, in 1900 or thereabouts, to eventually farm in the crater and to conclude the first phase of his plan by building up a large cattle herd for the historic trek, is a very good question. His initial reactions on first sight of this grandiose, game-filled paradise – probably whilst on a prospecting or hunting trip – would undoubtedly have been similar to those of a visitor today. That is: initially amazement and awe, and then appreciation of nature's lavish expanse of vastness, colour, and beauty.

*A wary lioness patrols the grasslands.*

Remember, however, that irrespective of his dabbling with chemistry, prospecting, hunting, and other fields of interest, Adolf Siedentopf originated from a long line of shrewd and experienced farmers who were close to the land. After the initial feeling of personal insignificance in the face of the magnificent panorama of scenery, fauna, and flora, he would have scrutinized the crater with a farmer's practical eye.

Other than the Lerai Forest, approximately 2.6 kilometres (1 mile) square, and the lake, the floor of the Ngorongoro covers some 260 square kilometres (100 square miles) of high-quality grazing land on open, slightly undulating plains. Adolf will have also noticed first-class permanent water at the Lemunge River, the Lerai stream, and other springs and rivulets. The soda lake, Lake Magadi, and nearby salt deposits provided natural licks to keep livestock in good condition in a tropical country. He would also have discovered that the crater floor at about 1,740 metres (5,700 feet) and its rim at 2,280 metres (7,500 feet) above sea level provided a healthy, invigorating climate. Oldeani Mountain, together with the adjacent thick forest to the east, helps establish a good seasonal rainfall, and the comparatively cool climate and open country discourages many of the indigenous cattle diseases. Importantly, the crater floor was free of the dreaded tsetse fly which would infect and decimate the cattle.

He would have noted that the only real disadvantages were the Maasai and Wanderobo permanently resident there, and the lion population. Undoubtedly he would have passed these off as easily controllable, and concentrated on the biggest advantage to him in farming there: he would be completely isolated in a kingdom of his own making, well away from the civilization so abhorrent to him. Well off the beaten track at the time, with no access roads, the Ngorongoro was 100 kilometres (60 miles) from the nearest government outpost at Mbulu and 180 kilometres (110 miles) from Arusha, the main northern administrative centre. The crater must have represented Utopia for this giant reclusive farmer.

The Siedentopf brothers made themselves a temporary tented base camp on the Lemunge River at the north end of the crater, where they later constructed Farm Soltau, a typical German-style farmhouse with stores and outbuildings. Present-day visitors can still see the remains of this site.

The first priority was to build strong cattle stockades from thorn trees to protect the cattle from the Maasai and lions. Fredrich then built himself a similar farmholding called Teichof (sometimes known as Laroda) in the Lerai Forest, at the south-eastern end of the crater, where the present research cabin is situated.

The German archaeologist Professor Hans Reck, mentioned at the beginning of this book, visited Farm Soltau and its inhabitants in 1911, and we are indebted to him for the only detailed description of the buildings. Reck recorded in his book *Oldoway*,

*The green, well-watered plains of the Ngorongoro, so attractive to the Siedentopfs.*

*die Schlucht des Urmenschen* (Olduvai, the Gorge of Prehistoric People) that before meeting Adolf he had heard the most fascinating stories about him. From Tanga, on the coast, to Arusha he was renowned as the 'feared, unapproachable King of the Ngorongoro'. He wrote that 'He had the reputation of throwing every traveller out of the crater.' He later added: 'I put a revolver in my pocket before introducing myself to Adolf'!

He found Farm Soltau to be a homely-looking, typical German farmhouse, with a thatched grass roof and a circular Arabic entrance. Horse heads were carved on the ends of the roof gables, and neat, well-built stores and stables, roofed with corrugated iron, surrounded the house.

'An enormous person seemed to completely fill the house entrance. This was Adolf, dressed in khaki clothes, with two rows of cartridge loops on his bush jacket.' As soon as Adolf discovered that Reck was not a government official 'intruding on his property', he was very friendly and hospitable. Adolf became a good friend and did all he could to assist Reck with his Olduvai research.

Typical of the giant recluse's attitude towards officialdom was a large nail on the wall of his lounge, stacked with unopened government letters that were impaled on it. As a settler myself in the old colonial days I feel envious of Adolf's simple answer to officialdom!

Understandably, the Maasai took strong exception to the white men, their askaris, and their livestock encroaching on their own domain, and strived, without success, to kill the interlopers and steal their cattle. In his African game stories published by his niece, Ursula Oetker, Adolf gives little mention of his early days in the crater and the constant war with the Maasai. Certainly a considerable number of Maasai moran warriors would have been killed or wounded during those troubled, hectic days whilst the brothers were building up their farms.

When I first started researching the Ngorongoro background in the 1950s from my coffee farm next to the crater, I knew several African old-timers who had worked for the Siedentopfs. These included Maganga ya Nyoka (Swahili for 'the Snake Doctor') who was semi-retired and worked for me as a gardener. He was a fascinating individual from the Wasukuma tribe, originating from near Lake Victoria. The Wasukuma are completely unafraid of all snakes, even the most poisonous varieties, and still use snakes for their dances and traditional ceremonies. Although we had a Lutheran mission hospital nearby, if a snake bit any of the local people, they would always go to Maganga for treatment rather than the hospital. Providing there was a spark of life, Maganga invariably cured him by using antidotes made from the roots of forest trees, and nobody, including myself, was ever allowed to watch him preparing the *dawa* (medicine).

Maganga had no idea which year he started working for Adolf Siedentopf, but did remember that the brothers were still living in tents when he joined them. This would have been about 1907.

*Adolf Siedentopf prepares to shoot the wounded leopard attacking Maganga ya Nyoka (this page).*

Maganga told me, 'The Maasai and Wanderobo made war against the bwanas, often attacking at night to try and kill them and steal cattle.' He could not remember Adolf himself ever shooting to kill or wound any of his attackers as he 'fired over their heads to scare them'. If he captured them, however, Maganga said he would flog them with a *kiboko* (hippo skin whip) in order to teach them a lesson.

'Sometimes the cattle askaris who guarded the cattle shot at and killed the Maasai.' This was an interesting remark, as Adolf's askaris were also Maasai, though of a different clan to the crater Maasai.

Employed primarily as personal gun bearer and game tracker to Adolf, Maganga had many battle scars to show for his occupation. These included a 10-centimetre (4-inch) wound on top of his head, and another on his foot, which were inflicted when a leopard wounded by Adolf sprang on him. He recounted, 'The bwana killed him with a final shot whilst he was eating me'!

Maganga also assisted the Siedentopfs to construct their houses and outbuildings, and was present when one of their managers, Rothe, excavated the Neolithic gravesites near Adolf's house. 'Bwana Adolf was a good bwana but very *kali* (severe). He whipped me once when I forgot to have spare cartridges ready for his gun when a wounded elephant charged us. He killed it near Engaruka and it had very big tusks. When we

*Maganga ya Nyoka in 1952, displaying his skills with a python.*

climbed the Rift wall to go back to camp it took two men to carry each tusk.' Judging by the description of the ivory, this must have been a very large elephant, with each tusk weighing anything between 55 and 68 kilograms (120 and 150 pounds). The Siedentopfs shot many elephant, selling the ivory to buy supplies and farm equipment in Arusha, 160 kilometres (100 miles) away. Until a wagon trail was cleared, the tusks would have had to be physically carried. Maganga helped the brothers build this trail. 'It followed an old elephant track through the forest and we only had to widen it in spots by removing trees', Maganga recalls.

The trail passed through Nainokanoka, following a centuries-old, wide elephant trail through what is now the Northern Highlands Forest Reserve (NHFR) above the Karatu and Oldeani farms. It met the escarpment of the Great Rift Valley just above Engaruka, where the wagons had to be dismantled and lowered down the precipitous slope to the floor of the valley. This necessary trail opened up the Ngorongoro district to the rapidly expanding centre of Arusha, and resulted in the Siedentopfs having closer contact with civilization, thus disturbing their self-enforced solitude at the crater.

Maganga was present at the many *barazas* (meetings) of the Siedentopfs with the Maasai elders, which led to an eventual uneasy truce between the two parties, with the moran still trying to steal cattle, but with fewer attempts on the lives of the white men. I employed mostly local Wambulu tribesmen and one of them, Tlatlaa Saidi, also worked for the Siedentopfs before the First World War. He remembered Adolf obtaining permission from government just before the war to import six four-shot magazine shotguns. 'A single-shot shotgun was useless for the askaris defending the cattle at night – several Maasai would attack at one point at the same time. There was only one shot with the old guns and there was no time to reload.'

Reluctantly, but inevitably, the Maasai, who attach a great amount of importance to fighting and physical strength, built up a respect for the giant, blue-eyed, fair-haired white men who lived in their midst, and whom they found to be too tough and resourceful to drive out of the crater.

Meanwhile, although this was comparatively healthy cattle country, the Siedentopfs often suffered big losses before finding answers to the different forms of cattle sickness and other livestock diseases. Pedigree cattle, sheep, and goats imported from Germany to cross-breed with local stock often died before they had a chance to build up immunity to these diseases.

Until 1907, Adolf was farming in the Ngorongoro by 'squatter's rights'. That is, he had roughly surveyed for himself an initial 6,500 hectares (16,000 acres) of land there, started farming without a land title, and then notified the authorities where he was and what he was doing, and placed a request for title deeds. Once Adolf's homestead was

*Maasai moran warrior.*

*Paula Siedentopf with her tame cheetah at Farm Soltau on the crater floor.*

*Picture courtesy of Mike Leach*

*The fort at Arusha, 200 kilometres (120 miles) from the Siedentopfs and their nearest military and administrative centre. It is now the military museum in Arusha.*

*Margaret Trappe, an outstanding hunter and tracker.*

established and Fredrich's camp had been built, Fredrich also applied for rights of occupancy for some 3,000 hectares (7,500 acres) of land.

For a time the administration left them to their own devices but in August 1907 one of the most famous of the pioneer German professional hunters, Bast, guided a Land Commission agent from Arusha to the crater in order to establish, if necessary, the Siedentopf's legal land title. It is not surprising that up to that time the brothers had been left to their own devices, as African messengers from the administrative centre at Arusha took at least six days to deliver correspondence to the nearest government base to the crater, at Mbulu. Messages took a further three or four days from Mbulu to Ngorongoro, 100 kilometres (60 miles) away, passing through game-infested country.

Earlier that year the Siedentopfs and the crater Maasai had attended a Lands Commission meeting at Moshi, the main German administrative centre in the north, located at the foot of Mount Kilimanjaro, 240 kilometres (150 miles) east of Ngorongoro. The brothers' applications for land titles were turned down because they had failed to show evidence of a reasonable amount of capital available for official surveying and development of the land they were squatting on. The Maasai, who lived in a solitary boma on the floor of the crater, were also refused permission to stay there 'because of their stealing', and they were allocated new pastureland for their cattle elsewhere in the Maasai Reserve.

The Land Commission agent accompanying Bast saw the nature and size of the Siedentopfs' farming development, and consequently Adolf was granted a 25-year lease on his farm. The property was then surveyed and demarcated with beacons. Fredrich's application for rights of occupancy, or a title deed, for his adjoining farm was, however, turned down, as at the time he had done little to develop his land and was instead fast establishing himself more as a hunter than a farmer.

The Maasai made even more determined efforts after this to drive the Siedentopfs out. When they failed to do so by spear and simi they resorted to starting widespread bushfires in an attempt to burn them out of the area.

Once Adolf was granted his 25-year lease he forged ahead with farm development, improving his indigenous cattle with imported bulls, experimenting with the cross-breeding of sheep, planting wheat, sisal, maize, and barley, buying horses, and planting clover for improved pasture.

Present-day visitors are often surprised to see clover there. He even started a canning factory for such delicacies as buffalo and wildebeest tongues, for export to a select but enthusiastic market back in Germany. As late as the 1930s it was still possible to see the old factory on the farm site. In order to expand his farm operations he found it necessary to employ supervisors, and within a short period he had several European assistants,

*Margaret Trappe winning a rather unusual bet (opposite page).*

*A donkey immediately regrets kicking Adolf Siedentopf (opposite page).*

*Paula Siedentopf being carried ashore on her arrival at Tanga.*

seldom numbering less than four. They included his brother-in-law Meyer, Gustav Rose, Stenzel, Rothe, and Freund.

During one of his infrequent trips to Arusha in 1911 Adolf, now 39 years old and appearing to be set for a bachelor's life, courted and married a German girl called Paula Meyer. They met at his friend Trappe's farm, in Arusha. Margaret Trappe, then a young girl, was a close friend of mine and was the first of only two ladies ever to be licensed as professional hunters in East Africa. An outstanding hunter, she served with General von Lettow-Vorbeck's army, fighting against the British and Allied troops in the First World War. For a bet she once chalked *pumbafu* (Swahili for 'idiot') on the back of a sleeping rhino – another example of the boldness of an extraordinary woman of that time!

Paula, aged 27, was to be thrown into the deep end, as far as her future was concerned, when they spent their one-month honeymoon on safari through Maasailand in an ox cart! Her husband warned her that she would often have to be by herself at the crater and insisted that she should learn to handle a rifle efficiently. He took her out lion hunting. Paula's niece, Ursula, recorded that on the first occasion her aunt tried to shoot a lion she missed it completely. On the second occasion she managed to shoot and kill the lion – 'I was more scared of Adolf than the lion, if I missed!'

Shortly afterwards her brother, Ferdinand Meyer, came out from Germany to join them at the crater. He was as tall and as powerfully built as Adolf. When he arrived at the crater both his sister and Adolf were out, riding separately around the farm checking the livestock. Adolf was the first to return. After they introduced themselves, these two enormous men started a friendly fight to see who was the stronger! When Paula returned she found, to her horror, her husband and her brother rolling around the floor having a first class set-to! 'It was the start of a big friendship', she wrote.

Life in the remote crater, with no female companionship, and more than 160 kilometres (100 miles) from the nearest shops and civilization, must have been very lonely for Paula. She eventually found it impossible to be without female company, and young Eva Wenkel was engaged from Germany to become her companion. I was in correspondence with Eva in the 1960s when she lived in Berlin. At that time she appeared to be the sole surviving European of the pre-First World War pioneering days in the Ngorongoro.

Eva was 21 when she and Paula sailed from Germany to Tanga on the *Gertrude Woerman* in 1912. Adolf met them off the ship and they took 14 days to complete the ox wagon trip to the Ngorongoro. She found the trip to be an 'unforgettable journey', as well it must have been in the eyes of a young lady used to town life. Writing to me of her life in the crater, she remembered particularly the enormous bush fires, the wild native dances, and the roaring of the lions.

Surprisingly, although she heard the lions every night she never actually saw one. This meant that by 1912 the Siedentopfs had hunted the lion population so unmercifully in defence of their livestock that they stayed well away from the farms, though they remained on the crater floor to hunt and live off their natural game meat. The enormous numbers of wild animals occupying the crater were almost uncontrollable, as we shall see later, with the lions a constant menace. They often leapt over the high thorn bush stockades at night, slaughtering and wounding several cattle before being shot by the askaris.

'Adolf was an outdoors, nature-loving person who was completely in love with his work', said Eva. 'The wild bush life that he lived and his unfriendliness towards most visitors, particularly "governmenties", gave him a bad, exaggerated reputation in the colony, although he was, in fact, an open-hearted, happy man. Adolf was severe but very just towards his Africans. I can recall only one incident when he whipped a man, for theft. On another occasion, however, he lost his temper when a donkey kicked him and he killed it with one blow of his fist! Travelling by ox wagon as we did I feel quite superior when I hear of present-day safaris by car and plane.'

Eva found life at the Ngorongoro with the Siedentopfs too lonely for her, so she left the farm in 1913, together with one of the managers, Freund, and went to Dar es Salaam.

Whilst the Siedentopfs normally discouraged visitors, particularly government officials, and wished only to be left alone in a kingdom of their own making, they did occasionally make fellow farmers and hunters welcome.

One of the first visitors to the Siedentopf ranches was the aforementioned South African, Gert Fourie, under what was, shortly afterwards, an almost tragic circumstance. He recorded that in 1908 he took six days to walk from Arusha to the Ngorongoro where he found, 'to my surprise', the two brothers. His diary continued: 'The Siedentopfs were living in tents and had built bomas for their cattle. The crater was swarming with wildlife of all sorts, except elephant, for they were around the crater on the high points and on the eastern slopes called Oldeani. I stayed with them five days. After the five days we left the Siedentopfs. They gave me two Wanderobo (to help him find big-tusked elephant) who had been with them since they arrived at the crater. In those days there were wild bushmen (Wanderobo) all around the crater. There was no other native population anywhere else, the nearest being at Mbulu, 60 miles east.' At the time of Gert Fourie's comments, the Maasai had been forced to leave their boma in the crater one year previously by the administration. It would appear that his memory was at fault here, as there were plenty of other Maasai closer than 60 miles (100 kilometres) away.

The Wanderobo took Fourie up onto the Oldeani Mountain nearby, where he promptly shot two large elephants. He then climbed a tree to line up his sights for a killing shot at a third elephant that was partially concealed in thick bush. His gun bearer, standing beneath the tree, accidentally fired the spare rifle. The shot wounded Fourie in four places, entering below the knee, passing through the thigh and then continuing through his left hand before finally exiting his wrist! He was losing a lot of blood, and used improvised tourniquets to prevent himself from bleeding to death. His faithful Africans loaded him onto his donkey and supported him on the steep descent from the Oldeani Mountain at 3,200 metres (10,500 feet) in order to receive medical attention at the Siedentopf's farm. It is difficult to imagine what he must have endured during this journey. At the foot of the mountain they met a large caravan travelling from a gold mine to Arusha. They provided him with a litter and four porters and an army corporal to continue his descent down into the crater floor. The precipitous cattle track was so slippery that the corporal, who was wearing hobnailed boots, carried him on his back to Fredrich's house, only to find that he was away. Fourie was then transported by pony to Adolf's house, where fortunately there was a visiting German nurse.

'Adolf, who was as strong as any two men, lifted me out of the litter like a baby, took me into the house and gently put me down on a bed.' When showing me his diary, Gert Fourie's son pointed out a photo of his father, and he appeared to be a stocky, very heavily built man, so being 'lifted like a baby' gives some indication of Adolf's strength! Fourie recuperated there for the next fortnight, attended by the nurse, who undoubtedly saved his life – a life that, by no stretch of the imagination, can certainly be termed 'charmed'. He had been severely wounded in the Boer War and was afterwards hit by a charging rhino. These wounds partially crippled him so he was only able to walk short distances and resorted to riding a small white donkey for longer safaris.

Once he had recovered he left the Siedentopfs and started his return trip to Arusha. En route he met his wife near Engaruka. She had travelled over 160 kilometres (100 miles) through game-filled and only partially explored country by ox wagon from their farm, Kampfontein, near Arusha, accompanied by a few Africans, in order to find out what had happened to her husband. When they met she was so relieved she gave him hell for not returning earlier, and he had to wait for an opportunity to interrupt her and tell his story as well as showing her his wounds! Her rescue trip gives some idea of the mettle of the women of the pioneer settler South Africans.

It is impossible for me to write now at length of this amazing old Afrikaans hunter, Gert Fourie, as I would be accused, justifiably, of leading the reader astray off the crater track. It may, however, be of interest to the reader that in 1928 Fourie accompanied the Prince of Wales (Duke of Windsor) and Baron von Blixen on a safari as a professional hunter.

Returning to the Siedentopfs during 1908, it was about this time that the German government began to realize the great potential of the Ngorongoro as a game sanctuary and tourist attraction. Fortunately for the brothers, however, the administration had other, higher priorities. Opening up new settlement areas, completing rail links between towns, and crop experimentation came first, although game conservation was rapidly becoming increasingly important. Communications, land surveying, agricultural development, and building construction forged ahead at a rapid rate throughout the country in typically industrious German fashion.

It was during the immediate pre-First World War years, once the preservation of game had became a higher priority, that the administration realized its mistake in allowing the Siedentopfs to farm in the crater. Irrespective of the unfriendly attitude of the Siedentopfs towards other interested settlers who visited the crater, it was impossible for the brothers to prevent other Germans applying for land there. Several would-be settlers visited the crater once the wagon trail, opened by the Siedentopf brothers themselves, was completed, and seeing the excellent land and prospects there, also applied for farms. Once these applications were made the government was forced to take more interest in this remote corner of the country.

As soon as they realized the potential of the crater as a game park, as well as an ideal area for further farm development, the administration was faced with a dilemma. Should the whole of the crater and its surrounds be alienated for settlement or, alternatively, should it be consolidated as a game/tourist area?

The government's point of view was summed up perfectly later by D Jaeger, who surveyed and mapped the crater and its surrounds in 1912 for the governor, Schnee. Following several applications for farms and 'shooting box' rights, he wrote in his report: 'Should this unique game sanctuary be desolated for a few farms, with a few thousand cattle, when, in the whole of Africa, there is nowhere else where such a tremendous concentration of game species exists? The natural borders (the rim of the crater) would assist a lot with game control.'

The fate of the crater was at that time in the balance, as it was to be again later during the British administration.

The German government decided that it had made a mistake originally in allowing Adolf rights of occupancy on his Farm Soltau. They recognized him as a first-class settler, albeit a difficult customer with regards to relations with the administration. They also respected and admired him as an intrepid pioneer who, in spite of constant troubles with cattle thieves, diseases, and predatory animals, was making a success of his farming enterprise. However, he was farming, understandably, in the best section of the crater.

*He begins his desperate journey down the mountain to seek medical attention.*

*Gert Fowrie is accidentally shot by his own gun bearer (opposite page).*

*A lion and lioness shot by the Siedentopfs in the battle to defend their livestock from predation.*

*The 'horn' of the rhino is in fact made of keratin, a hairlike substance, and continues to grow during its lifetime.*

Historically it has been proven that it is extremely difficult, and in most cases impossible, for game preservation and farm development to operate side by side without destroying either or both.

Initially the government tried to buy Siedentopf out by offering compensation for the development he had made. Adolf refused. They then discovered an invidious fencing clause in his rights of occupancy which, strange to relate, was ultimately the deciding factor in the future of the crater nearly 30 years later, during the British occupation.

The development clause stipulated that his property should be fenced – an impossible condition which he should never have agreed to. The imagination boggles at the futile waste of effort and money Adolf would have spent constructing a 32-kilometre (20-mile) fence in a game-filled area, even though by that time Adolf was a very wealthy man, with 1,000 upgraded cattle, 2,500 sheep, 40 donkeys, and 12 horses. The fence would have been continually broken down by animals, even whilst being constructed.

Whilst Adolf's future was in doubt, the government made a clear-cut decision on his brother, Fredrich, due to his indifference to farming. He was using the farm, on which he was squatting, as a base from which to equip his hunting safaris. In 1912 the Mbulu district officer reported to Arusha that Fredrich had only '60 to 70 cows, about 12 hectares [30 acres] of wheat and maize, and his buildings consisted of a few mud huts'. Conversely, in an old German file, it was recorded that in 1913 he had 200 cattle, 500 sheep, 3 horses, 4 ploughs, 28 oxen, and 7.5 hectares (18 acres) of arable land. In 1912 Fredrich wrote an aggrieved letter to the German colonial secretary in Berlin after he had been told that he would be unable to establish a lease for his farm. He wrote: 'If I have to leave now I will lose five years of my life, irrespective of the cost of development.' He went on to say that he had a 'moral right' to remain in the crater after his years of pioneering and that, if necessary, he would taker the matter to the German president himself.

Meanwhile, it seems that a rift was beginning to appear between the two brothers as Fredrich, together with Gustav Rose, Adolf's ex-manager, had plans to turn Teichof, Fredrich's farm, into a 'shooting box'. Gustav Rose had also applied for a 15,000-hectare (37,000-acre) hunting concession on the west side of the crater. When he requested this shooting box Rose wrote to Governor Schnee that it was his intention to form a German East African hunting bureau with Fredrich Wilhelm, and that he intended to increase the 60,000 Deutschmark he had for this project to 100,000.

Back in Germany the Ngorongoro and its surrounds were fast becoming famous for the fantastic numbers and variety of game there. Fredrich was busy advertising with a professional hunting safari brochure. Bast had taken two royal princes of Bavaria there in 1912, and the trip was so successful that a considerable number of the German aristocracy were interested in booking and hunting the same location.

Although the shooting of rhino in the crater itself was forbidden by government decree, and Fredrich had failed to persuade them to lift the restriction, there were plenty of rhino available outside the Ngorongoro, many of them with phenomenally big horns. The second world record was shot in Oldeani at one of my neighbouring farms.

Lion trophies from there and the adjoining Serengeti were unsurpassed in Africa. The whole area abounded with record-size black-maned lions, which are a particular type of lion, and a number one trophy for the majority of hunters.

During that time there were large numbers of big-tusked elephant, including many 100-pounders, the trophy par excellence, with each tusk weighing over 100 pounds (45 kilograms). The last elephant Fourie shot on Oldeani Mountain had tusks that weighed over 150 pounds (68 kilograms) each.

Thousands of buffalo, including many with record-class horns, roamed the rim of the crater and the adjoining areas. The world record was collected near the crater in the 1970s.

The last of 'the Big Five', the leopard, still abounded on the crater rim and in the forest.

Finally, safari clients could hunt in the area eland, hartebeest, wildebeest, zebra, reedbuck, Grant's and Thomson's gazelles, ostrich, and other game. No wonder the Ngorongoro was fast becoming a hunter's Mecca! If it had not been for the outbreak of the First World War the Ngorongoro Crater would have been lost to posterity as a game sanctuary.

In May 1913 the governor, Schnee, wrote to the Arusha administration that it was impossible to declare the crater a national park because Adolf had turned down proffered compensation in return for leaving, and insisted on carrying on his farming venture there. Schnee intended recommending to Berlin that the whole area should be opened up, and that both Fredrich and Rose's applications for safari development be accepted. Fredrich and Rose had made personal visits to Schnee and managed to persuade him to adopt this line.

The Mbulu district officer, Haeger, and the Arusha administration, who knew the crater area, had already crossed swords with the Siedentopf brothers, and were vehemently opposed to Schnee's recommendation. They wanted to force the brothers out of the crater and proclaim the area a national park. The Arusha administration, having failed to persuade Adolf to accept compensation and move, were trying to apply the invidious fencing clause of the title deeds which Adolf had originally – no doubt with tongue in cheek! – agreed to.

*The big-tusked elephant of the Ngorongoro attracted many early hunters.*

*The impressive horns of the buffalo were also sought by trophy hunters.*

*The fertile volcanic soils of the Ngorongoro district make excellent farmland, a fact which has often give rise to land use conflicts during the area's chequered history.*

During 1913 Haeger wrote to the Arusha administrative headquarters that he had been informed that Adolf had commenced construction of the fence. The following year, 1914, he followed up with a second letter stating that the fence had in fact still not been erected. Adolf, very sensibly, was trying to persuade the government to agree that, once he had constructed the fence, the administration should pay him compensation for game breaking it and damaging his property, as he was prohibited to shoot game on the farm. This was a most important stipulation which, after the war, qualified lawyers failed to insist upon when the British government had an identical situation with Adolf's successor. There the matter rested for the time being.

Meanwhile, in early 1914, Fredrich Wilhelm took out his first professional hunting safari in the crater. It was very successful and he applied to the government for permission to recruit 200 Wasukuma and Wanyamwezi tribesmen to live in the crater and be employed on his expanding safari operations. These two tribes are formidable hunters and meat eaters. Unless rigorously controlled they would soon have made great inroads into the crater's game population.

He and Rose broke off their friendship, for reasons that are not recorded, and Rose applied for professional safari rights on 8,000 hectares (20,000 acres) of Crown land in the Oldeani/Karatu district. The application was turned down as the administration realized the great farming potential there. This decision was vindicated when the Oldeani district, which subsequently included my farm, was opened up for agriculture, primarily coffee, after the First World War.

The same year, just before the outbreak of war, there was a tremendous revival of interest in Germany for further excavation and investigation of the gravesites at Olduvai and the crater. Kattwinkel (who originally discovered Olduvai), Arning, Reck, and several other well-known archaeologists and geologists returned there.

Immediately prior to the war Adolf was still fighting against cattle diseases and Maasai rustlers, who had just stolen 150 head of cattle. At the same time his brother Fredrich was busy with his safari plans and had five big German safaris already booked for 1915. The government was prepared to alter a section of its game preservation legislation to allow private hunting concessions.

Then war was declared. This put paid to all decisive plans for the future of the Ngorongoro and, ironically, eventually saved the crater for posterity as the paradise for game preservation and conservation that it is today.

Fredrich immediately joined the army, leaving his livestock and farm possessions with his brother.

Adolf, well away from the various major battlefields where the British and German forces were fighting for supremacy, carried on farming, and for some time supplied the German army with livestock and canned food. One of the final entries in the old German files shows that Adolf, who had been fighting government protocol for so many years to establish a freehold title to his farm, had finally won. The title had been granted and awaited him at Mbulu for his signature. Conditions were very unsettled at the time and, ironically, Adolf was unable to make the trip.

Hans Reck records that he was present at the close of the Siedentopf phase of the crater's history. During 1916 Reck, who was then in the army, called at Adolf's house whilst there was a lull in the fighting near the crater. Adolf had just received orders to vacate the farm due to the approach of British troops. Reck and his askaris watched Adolf and the cattle drovers slowly driving the enormous herd of livestock which, by that time, comprised 1,200 cattle, 3,000 sheep, 15 horses, and 40 donkeys out of the crater and towards Oldeani. Within a few months, most of his stock had died of disease and Adolf was captured and shipped to India where he was interned until 1920.

It requires little imagination to picture how soul-destroying it must have been for this giant, outdoors-loving man, surrounded by thousands of fellow prisoners, and deprived of his freedom and privacy.

It was here, in an effort to at least release his mind from the cage, that Adolf painstakingly wrote his fascinating stories on game and tribal lore that were later published by his niece, Ursula Oetker. In spite of the thousands of books which have since been written on wildlife, his detailed accounts of their pattern of behaviour still rank among the few absolutely accurate manuscripts written by a first-class, self-taught naturalist. It should also be borne in mind that game was only a hobby with him, not a profession as it was, to a greater extent, with his brother Fredrich, added to which most of his time and energies were devoted to developing his farm. The unique position of the farm, however, surrounded and occupied by thousands of head of game, gave him an ideal opportunity over the years to study and observe the animals around him.

Adolf made a particular study of man-eating lions, and he had some very interesting theories concerning them. He wrote that the most prolific numbers of maneaters were found on the various old slave and caravan routes and on railway construction sites, particularly during the years 1897–98. This was when the sand flea (chigger), which burrows under the toenails to lay its eggs, invaded Africa, sweeping across the continent from the Atlantic to the Indian Ocean.

Thousands of otherwise strong people lay crippled on the caravan routes, slowly dying of blood poisoning, and were thus easy prey for the lions. Shortly before that, the Triple Plague of rinderpest, smallpox, and locusts had devastated large tracts of

Africa, killing hundreds of thousands of people through starvation and disease. The lions became used to a diet of human flesh, and their cubs thrived upon the human diet they had became accustomed to instead of their traditional game meat. They in turn passed on the acquired taste to their cubs.

At the turn of the century, whilst there were very large caravans and gangs of construction workers travelling upcountry with inadequate medical facilities, there was always a large percentage of deaths. Patterson writes about this in his book *Maneaters of Tsavo*, and gives horrific descriptions of what occurred.

The German government's answer to what had become a very serious menace was to offer a bounty of a certain amount per tail to people who killed lions, and they also sent out armed guards with the caravans. Eventually the majority of maneaters, particularly those in the worst trouble spots, such as around Lake Victoria, were killed off.

While Adolf was imprisoned in India and 'escaping' through his writing, his wife, Paula, stayed on a South African friend's farm during the war and, after the armistice, was allowed to return to her house in the crater, taking with her a small herd of livestock. In 1920 she was evicted from the farm and ordered by the British government to return to Germany on the last evacuation boat from Tanga.

Husband and wife were reunited in Hamburg the same year, and the niece records how helpless her uncle was in the city. On one occasion he became hopelessly lost, and had to be taken home by the police! Who cannot but feel sorry for this freedom-loving explorer and pioneer, bewildered and lost in the teeming population and traffic of an enormous city. Used to breaking new trails in the vastness of the African continent, using the stars and sun to guide him, and never losing himself, he was as helpless in civilization as a three-year-old child.

Adolf tried, unsuccessfully, to farm again in Germany, near Hamburg, but could not settle down to the comparatively crowded life and restrictions of a civilized country after tasting the sweet wildness of Africa. In a vain effort to recapture the life of the open spaces, he sold the farm in 1922 and emigrated to America in 1925.

Meanwhile he tried, unsuccessfully, to obtain compensation from the German government for the loss of his farm in the crater. He applied for over a million marks to cover, mostly, his livestock, and this represented a considerable fortune directly after the First World War.

'Did he get a penny? I don't think so', wrote his niece, although he did in fact receive compensation of £494 from the British government in 1925. If he had been successful with his claim from the German government, no doubt it would

*The noisy mating rituals of a pair of Ngorongoro lions.*

*A black-maned lion quenches its thirst at a freshwater pool.*

have been possible for him to find an enormous tract of land in America, or elsewhere, to satisfy his urge for the open spaces. Or he may even have returned to Africa.

Initially he joined a cousin on his farm in Montana, but Africa had thinned out his blood too much for him to be able to stand up to the cold climate there. In 1925 he bought his final farm in the warmer climate of Alabama and he died there in 1932 at the comparatively young age of 60. It is recorded that he died of a brain haemorrhage, but one wonders if a contributory cause was a 'broken heart', no mention of which is made in medical journals. War hits out indiscriminately, affecting all people from all walks of life, but possibly there is less pity than deserved for those civilians whose lives are completely uprooted, leaving them lost and lonely in a new, hated environment. Such a man was Adolf Siedentopf, 'the feared, unapproachable King of the Ngorongoro'.

During the war his brother, Fredrich, was captured and afterwards repatriated to Germany. There he married in 1921 and returned to Tanganyika with his wife in 1925. He started professional hunting again and also tried to obtain rights of occupancy for his old farm in the crater. 'I need the land to keep my safaris supplied with food', was his justification. The acting British governor turned down the application, most probably because the German files of the former administration showed that Fredrich had never legally owned the land.

Undeterred, he applied for a farm as close to his former farm as possible, in nearby Oldeani. He was successful with this application, and was one of the first predominately German settlers to be allocated land there. Shortly afterwards he sold his farm to my neighbour and friend, the late Carl Rhode. This is the last farm located on the right-hand side when leaving Oldeani towards the Ngorongoro.

He died in November 1931, possibly as a consequence of an air crash he was involved in when flying with the German fighter pilot ace of the First World War, Udet, on a film safari. They descended for a close shot of a pride of lions sitting on top of a termite hill in the crater, and the male leader of the pride took exception to this manoeuvre, reared up, and tore off the landing wheels, forcing it to crash-land. Both Udet and Fredrich were injured in the crash-landing.

His death closed the chapter of two of the Ngorongoro Crater's most colourful characters. Dressed in their safari clothes, with broad-brimmed terai hats, like stetsons, and mounted on their horses with a six-gun on the hip and a 9.3 Mauser rifle in its scabbard, they were truly 'cowboys in Africa'.

*Fredrich Siedentopf's plane was forced to crash-land after the wheels were torn off in a low pass over a pride of lions (this page).*

*Harry Hurst's somewhat unusual technique for photographing a bull hippo (page 86).*

*Zebra and flamingo share the alkaline waters of Lake Magadi.*

*Vultures flock to a kill on the Ngorongoro grasslands.*

*A lioness and its cubs bask in the morning sun.*

*Buffalo populations fluctuate with disease and animal movements, but they are currently numerous within the crater.*

*Despite its size the eland is a graceful antelope. It wanders widely and has a very varied diet.*

*Baboons leaping across a watercourse.*

*Adult and young black rhino.*

# The Crater Becomes a Scots Baronet's Shooting Box

After the First World War the League of Nations declared Tanganyika a trusteeship territory to be administered by the British government. All former German-owned properties, with a few isolated exceptions, were taken over by a newly formed government department, known as the Custodian of Enemy Property (CEP). They were then either sold at public auction or allocated to young ex-servicemen who applied for them.

During the Second World War, during which there was no actual warfare in Tanganyika between the Germans and the Allies, most German farm owners were interned and their farms continued production under the management of the CEP. After the war young ex-servicemen were encouraged to apply for the farms again and, in 1948, under this category, I was successful in obtaining, out of 25 applicants, the farm I then called 'Shangri-La'.

Returning to post-First World War days. Since neither of the Siedentopf farms had a registered title deed, this was the ideal opportunity for the British government to start a completely fresh sheet on the subject of the Ngorongoro, and immediately and irrevocably ensure the future of the crater as a national park or reserve.

All they had to do was to declare Adolf Siedentopf's farm, Soltau, Crown property, and then complete the necessary formalities. A great number of old German files were available that dealt with the former government's efforts to expel the Siedentopf brothers from the crater in order to declare the whole area a game sanctuary.

As we have seen, there had been plenty of pressure on Governor Schnee to evict Adolf Siedentopf and include his farm in a game reserve. Schnee, however, recognized him as an excellent farmer, and respected him for his success in turning a completely isolated corner into a first-class farm, despite the many handicaps. It was for these reasons that he decided, in 1913, 'in all fairness', not to expel Adolf, but to alienate the whole crater for farming development together with a safari bureau.

After the First World War, however, the British government were not in the same predicament as Schnee, since Soltau had been confiscated as ex-enemy property without title, and Adolf was incarcerated in a camp in India at the time.

There were also plenty of pre-war settlers of non-German background in Tanganyika, particularly around Arusha, who knew the background of the crater and the struggle the former German government had in attempting to take over the area as a game sanctuary. Regrettably, there was no effort by the British government to utilize this local knowledge, and the ideal opportunity for an immediate decision to declare Farm Soltau as Crown land, and establish the Ngorongoro as a national park, had been missed. This would have saved tens of thousands of hours of wasted time, expense, and effort over the controversial future of the crater during the next 40 years.

*A pair of zebras make an interesting artistic pattern in black and white.*

*A baby zebra, still unsteady on its feet, is suckled by its mother.*

*Thomson's gazelle and wildebeest, common inhabitants of the Ngorongoro Conservation Area.*

Up to as recently as 1959 the future of the crater was still undecided. Even to this day it is not a national park devoted solely to wildlife, but has became a conservation authority area, where the interests of the Maasai and game are shared.

The first mistake made by the new British administration was to allow Adolf's wife, Paula, to return to Farm Soltau after the war, and continue farming there until 1920 whilst her husband was imprisoned. This magnanimous gesture unfortunately had the effect of renewing interest in a possible re-alienation of the old farming land.

Possibly Paula had been allowed back to the farm as Adolf was a civilian during the war and had not fought against the British. However, had that been the case, the Siedentopfs may have been permitted to purchase their farm back for a nominal sum, as happened in several cases with German farm owners after the Second World War. Several of the farms next to mine in Oldeani, which were owned by Germans interned during the Second World War, were returned after the war.

It was in 1920 that the government forced Paula to vacate the farm, and, as we have seen, she returned to Germany and rejoined her husband. Certainly the eviction was not made with the intention of keeping the crater clear of settlement as in 1919 a Captain Harry Hurst, ex-British Army, had been allowed to squat on Fredrich's old farm, Teichof. Harry Hurst was allowed officially to rent the property during his four-year stay there, and established in this short period a great reputation for himself as a naturalist, hunter, and photographer. According to comments made by people who met him he was completely fearless, and although digressing slightly from the subject at hand, I am sure the reader who has experienced wildlife in Africa will find some of the tales quite extraordinary.

The calibre of this ex-soldier may be judged by what the author F Radcliffe Holmes had to say of him in his book *Interviewing Wild Animals*. He dedicated his book to 'Harry Hurst, the finest man I have ever met'.

Holmes joined Hurst for several weeks in the crater, where Hurst was 'carrying on a little desultory farming and donkey breeding. The pursuit and study of big game, particularly the latter, was his ruling passion, and his knowledge of the wilds surpassed that of any other hunter, amateur or professional, I have ever met', wrote Holmes.

He then went on to give details of Harry Hurst's photographic technique. If he wanted a photograph of a lion, he would quietly track it to where it was dozing under a bush or in the grass. Then, when a few yards away, he would set up his camera and whistle or shout. 'The startled lion usually jumped up in a fright, stared incredulously at the intruder long enough to enable him to get his exposure and then, in most cases, turned and fled. If not, Hurst was always ready for it by the time it decided to charge and he was the surest shot I ever met.'

His method of photographing hippo might also be classified as foolhardy but was certainly very effective. There was an old bull hippo in the crater lake that Hurst had tried often, but in vain, to approach for a close shot. One day when the whole school of a dozen or so hippo were lounging in the middle of the lake, Hurst waded in, pushing an ancient dugout canoe in front of him. This provoked the old bull to promptly leave his companions and charge the photographer. When it was a yard or so away, Hurst calmly pushed the canoe into the cavern of its mouth and got his photo while the hippo was recovering from the surprise, and angrily chewing the not very appetizing morsel! Before it was ready to attack, its tormentor had retreated into shallow water where the irate monster was not anxious to follow him.

'This I know sounds a tall tale but the photo in question was seen by hundreds of people at the first Empire Exhibition at Wembley, though in all probability the story of how is was obtained has not previously been told in print, except by myself', writes Holmes.

Holmes's description of Hurst's technique for catching a young elephant he intended to send to the London Zoo is an even better illustration of his daredevil methods. He stalked into a large herd, waited patiently until he saw what he wanted, then dived into their midst, seizing by the tail a very young calf that 'seemed to have mislaid its mother'. What the calf said can be imagined! He said it very loudly too and the marvel was that the mother did not come to its rescue and pulverize the assailant. Hurst half carried and half pushed the calf back to the farm where, not long after, it was following him around like a dog. Unfortunately the calf later died because of the impossibility of supplying it with the correct diet.

The government then called in a number of expert hunters to deal with a herd of elephant raiding African maize fields in the Kilwa region at the coast, and Hurst joined the expedition. The last elephant he shot managed, in its death throes, to smash him against a tree, trampling and mortally wounding him.

The same year as his death, 1923, Hurst had been recommended by the Lands and Mines Department to be granted the 1,200 hectares (3,000 acres) he had applied for on Fredrich Wilhelm Siedentopf's old farm. Amazingly the department, knowing full well that the farm Teichof had never, officially, been owned by Adolf's brother, was prepared to allocate to Hurst 1,200 hectares of what was undeniably Crown land.

This, second, large mistake made by the government was compounded by a third and even bigger, far-reaching decision that caused tremendous trouble for years afterwards, and also put the crater at risk as a game sanctuary.

During 1921 a Scots baronet, Sir Charles Ross, the inventor of the renowned rifle bearing his name, visited the Ngorongoro on a shooting safari. T A Barns, the author,

*Milling herds seem almost dwarfed by the incomparable vistas of the Ngorongoro.*

*Elephants forage in the acacia groves of the Lerai Forest. An adult can eat as much as 200 kilograms (440 lbs) of vegetation in a day.*

*A reposing lion takes a fleeting interest in its photographer.*

*The lion population of the Ngorongoro averages about a hundred.*
*Their favoured prey are wildebeest and zebra.*

joined the safari and fully describes the expedition in his book *Across the Great Craterland to the Congo*. It was a grandiose safari with 150 porters and included Ross, Barns and his wife, the 'Major', an anonymous young lady 'DL', and Ross's chauffeur, Alec.

Barns, not unlike Baumann and all subsequent first-time visitors, was completely overawed by his first sight of the crater. We can gather this by his description: 'By reason of its vastness, and its novel surroundings, it far surpasses, in my opinion, such sights as Kili [Kilimanjaro] or the Mountains of the Moon, or even the great Kivu volcanoes. Of such a place one might well say, "See it and die", for surely no place was half as beautiful.'

What was to occur on this safari was nothing short of a massacre. DL shot a rhino the first day at the crater when it lay down to sleep 250 yards from the camp, and Barns then left his companions there to spend eight days 'looking around' on his own. When he returned to camp, he found that three black-maned lions had fallen to the party, and, during the next few days, DL and Ross shot a further seven lions and three cheetahs. Ross and Alec shot a lion and lioness in a charge that had been 'driven' by Maasai warriors. Ross then encountered what he described as a 'troop' (pride) of lions, near some 'underground lairs'. He killed one of the lions and wounded three others, 'but as the latter disappeared into some burrows, he was unable to retrieve them'. On departing from the crater, DL and Ross bagged one further rhino apiece.

From this account made by Barns, one can deduce that the Ross party was responsible for at least thirteen dead lions, three wounded ones, three or more rhino, and other game during their short safari in the crater. Only one lioness is mentioned in this account 'in charge', but there is no doubt that several other 'lions' were in fact lionesses!

As a professional hunter I deplore the conduct and indiscriminate shooting on this safari – please note that I deliberately use the term 'shooting' and not 'hunting'. No true hunter shoots lionesses, and the idea of using Maasai to 'drive' lions onto guns, similar to beaters at a partridge shoot, is illegal, unethical, and inexcusable! It would also appear that no effort was made to put the three wounded lions in the 'burrows' out of their misery – yet another inexcusable act.

Sir Charles Ross was so impressed by the variety and numbers of game animals in the crater, particularly the lions and rhinos, that he applied for a lease of Adolf Siedentopf's old farm, Soltau. Surprisingly, as with Hurst's application, and bearing in mind the vast tourist potential of the area, the government approved his application in 1922, and he only paid £4,700, at five shillings and ninepence an acre, for the some 16,000 acres (6,500 hectares)!

Following Hurst's death, Ross also applied for Fredrich's farm, Teichof, and it appears, from the records available, that he would have liked to purchase the entire crater.

The government then put up an auction notice stating: 'Aug 7, 1924, Laroda [Teichof], comprising some 1,500 acres, will be put up for auction. The yearly rental to be -/50 Cents an acre.' Fortunately, at the last moment, they decided to cancel the proposed auction, otherwise Ross, who was a very wealthy man, would have outbid any other interested parties and combined the two farms.

Ross installed four African caretakers on his new farm, Soltau, and obtained permission for them to have a shotgun to protect his property. One of the caretakers, Mohamed bin Ahmed, was a Somali who had accompanied Ross on his safari. Mohamed was paid 300 shillings (about £15) a month for his not excessive duties, and it would indeed be astonishing if he did not augment this, at that time, handsome salary by poaching! The clause, which has always existed in the Game Preservation Ordinance, allows a property owner or his representative to shoot game 'in defence of life and property'. This term covers a multitude of sins, particularly in a remote, game-filled area where there is little, if any, Game Department supervision, so the mind boggles at what may have happened in the area during Ross's time there!

After taking over Soltau, the reason given by his agent for Ross's application for the purchase of the remainder of the crater was: 'It is my client's intention to run a small experimental farm to determine what crops can be grown.' The Siedentopfs had already successfully grown wheat, maize, barley, sisal, and other crops, and Ross had not attempted to experiment with any crops at all since his purchase of Soltau. It would therefore appear extremely unlikely that farming was ever intended.

On the contrary: from the evidence of the considerable number of animals shot by the Ross party on his first safari and subsequent safaris, it was quite obvious that he wanted the Ngorongoro purely as his own private 'shooting box'. He lived thousands of miles away, in Scotland, and had no intention of living permanently in the crater.

The British government bitterly regretted the hasty transaction after the sale of Soltau. Fortunately the mistake was realized before any further land allocations, including Hurst's old farm, were made to Ross or anyone else.

Ross was determined to obtain freehold title rights for his 'farm', and his agent in Kenya made repeated representations over the years to the governor of Tanganyika, with the intention that the whole of the crater be alienated to his client.

It was at this stage that the government, like the pre-war German government, finally recognized that the Ngorongoro Crater would be ideal for a national park, with game sacrosanct. They found the same loophole in the Soltau title deeds as their predecessors, requiring Ross to either fence the property or vacate it. The title deeds Ross had for his farm were an exact duplicate of the documents the German administration had given Adolf Siedentopf. The only development clause imposed on the lease was the fencing of

*The eland is perhaps the most majestic of the antelopes.*

*A black rhino, clearly showing the prehensile lip used to browse on leaves and shoots. Oxpeckers search for ticks on its body.*

certain boundaries, 'on the fulfilment of which the lessee is entitled to the right of freehold'. The right of the government to terminate the lease was contained in the following clause: 'The contract of lease is concluded for an unspecified period as from April 1, 1907. The contracting parties may terminate the contract at the end of a calendar quarter by giving three months previous notice. Notice on the part of the lessee to terminate shall be given in a period of 25 years, i.e. not before March 31, 1932. Should the lessee be unable to fulfil his obligations in accordance with this contract, the lessor shall be entitled to give notice of immediate termination. If the contract be cancelled the lessee shall not be entitled to claim compensation for the outlay incurred.'

The matter was left pending for years, and involved reams of correspondence between Ross, his Kenya agent, the governor of Tanganyika, and many other very senior officials, including the secretary of state for the colonies.

Finally, in 1927, the director of game preservation (nowadays called chief game warden), C P M Swynnerton, introduced the first firm proposal for the future of the Ngorongoro. 'This [the crater] is a wonderful game reserve which, if made into an actual reserve, will one day be as famous as Yellowstone Park, and preserve in perpetuity in a readily visible condition a remnant of "old Africa". I am including it as a reserve in the draft ordinance and I would particularly ask that no more land be allocated in or beside it till that ordinance is considered, in case it should then be agreed to accept my recommendation with regard to it.'

Both Swynnerton and his son, Gerry, who was also chief game warden until his death in 1959, did a truly commendable amount of constructive work in the preservation of Tanganyika's game, and the above report confirms him as a man with a vision – similar to Jaeger, the German map maker, 15 years before.

Three years after the report was submitted, in 1930, Major R Hingston, representing the Society for the Preservation of the Fauna of the Empire, visited the crater. He too made strong recommendations that the Ngorongoro should become a national park.

The government continued to press for the fencing of the property and the agent for Ross contested the clause as being 'too costly and impractical'.

There was an interesting interview between the Kenya agent and the governor of Tanganyika. The agent made strong representations for his client to take over the whole of the crater to use both as an experimental farm and game reserve. The governor pointed out that since Ross was already fighting the fencing clause he could hardly open up an experimental farm without fencing it off from the prolific numbers of game.

The agent then tried a different approach and said that, if successful with his application for the whole of the crater, his client wished to turn it into a 'combined Yellowstone National Park and Simla [sanatorium]'. It was pointed out to him that the preservation of game was a government consideration and not private enterprise.

The agent's final gambit was that the Ngorongoro might be declared a game reserve, but then 'did not appear keen' on the suggestion that the area already purchased by Ross might also be included in the reserve. If this last proposal had been agreed, it would of course have prevented any further safaris by Ross or his friends hunting in the crater.

Needless to say, it was quite obvious to the governor that, above all other considerations, Sir Charles Ross wanted to try and retain shooting box rights there solely for himself and his successors.

The next major move by the government occurred when the draft ordinance proposed by the chief game warden became law, proclaiming the whole of the crater outside the boundaries of Soltau, which was still privately owned land, a game-protected area. This effectively stymied the several Arusha residents who had applied for farming land elsewhere in the crater, including the application from Fredrich Wilhelm Siedentopf to occupy his old farm, Teichof.

With the threat of eviction from Soltau by the government on the basis of the fencing clause, Ross's agent even reached the stage of making inquiries regarding costs of erecting a fence around the 6,500-hectare (16,000-acre) property. Some idea of the fantastic amount of material and, by present-day standards, comparatively low cost of this mammoth project can be gathered by the quotation from Mercier and Green, a general merchant store in Arusha:

| Approx. figures for fencing a total length of 20 miles with a five-strand, eight-gauge wire fence: | |
|---|---|
| Galvanized iron wire, with a breaking strain of 1,125 lbs., 360 rolls at Shs 18/- ............................................................. | 6,480 |
| Pillars, double winding with sole plates, 195 at Shs 50/-........... | 9,750 |
| Corner standards, 5 at Shs 60/-...................................... | 300 |
| 5,070 angle standards at Shs 2/25................................. | 11,400 |
| Approx. weight, 56 tons, cost of transport, approx................ | 2,500 |
| Fencing installation contract at £40 a mile (i.e. £800)........…... | 16,000 |
| Total estimated cost...................................................... | Shs 46,430 |

The £ was then worth 20 shillings, so the total cost would have been £2,320.

At this stage, therefore, Ross could have converted the leasehold title, which was beginning to run out, to a freehold title, thus retaining his 6,500 hectares (16,000 acres) of shooting rights, for the cost of about £2,300!

He refused, however, to invest this money in a development which would, admittedly, be impossible to maintain, with enormous numbers of animals continually breaking the

*Among the herbivores of the Ngorongoro, zebra are outnumbered only by wildebeest.*

fence down. Ross's agent slipped up very badly by failing to consider the completely relevant query raised originally by the previous owner, Adolf Siedentopf. Siedentopf asked the government if they would pay compensation for game breaking the fence and damaging the property.

The British government seemed reluctant to apply the penalty of forfeiture of his land if Ross failed to carry out the fencing. This was probably attributable to the great sense of fairness that, irrespective of its other alleged shortcomings, the government was always renowned for during the heyday of the Empire.

Everybody realized that, with the continual infiltration of masses of animals, particularly during the annual migration, the original fencing clause was ridiculous. If, however, Ross had indeed gone through the motions of fencing his property, his freehold title would have been granted and the crater would have been, virtually, partially privately owned up to 1963.

It was in 1963, two years after independence, that the African government of Tanganyika passed an amendment to the Lands Law, cancelling all freehold titles. Properties with former freehold titles were, however, normally converted to a 99-year lease. This could, theoretically, have resulted in Ross's successors retaining the Ngorongoro Crater farm until AD 2062!

Meanwhile, an ever-increasing number of tourists visited the crater during the period 1920 to 1930. Game lovers and game preservation societies throughout the world applied increasing pressure for the Ngorongoro to be proclaimed a national park so that the game might be preserved for posterity. Although the crater, with the exception of the farm, had been declared a game reserve, the area was too isolated to protect the game adequately.

It was not until 1931 that the stretch of main road from the Great North Road at Makiyuni to Oldeani was completed, linking Arusha to Oldeani. However, there still remained a further 16 kilometres (10 miles) or so to link up Oldeani with the crater. The Serengeti plains, now a national park, were an open hunting area at the time, and a steadily increasing number of hunters were attracted to the area, primarily for the famous black-maned lions. This meant their safaris passed the crater, and it is beyond the realms of probability that there was no indiscriminate hunting in the crater reserve en route!

1929 saw a new section of the Land Ordinance become law, and it offered the possibility of a solution to the seemingly everlasting wrangling between Ross and the government regarding the fencing clause. It read: 'The Governor may at his discretion and with the consent of the lessee substitute for the fencing condition a condition requiring improvement of any nature to a value not exceeding Shs 5/- an acre.' This section may

*The rising sun starts to clear the early morning mist shrouding Lake Magadi.*

*Large flocks of lesser flamingo sift the alkaline waters of Lake Magadi for the minute algae and diatoms that constitute their diet.*

*Wildebeest are extremely gregarious while in migration.*

*A lion cools itself in a stream.*

*The giraffe uses its long neck to browse on tender acacia shoots.*

well have been added to the ordinance in order to provide a face-saver for both parties in the Ngorongoro dispute.

There followed further correspondence between Ross's agent and the government, both trying to force the other to suggest an 'alternative development'. Five shillings an acre for improvements would have meant an expenditure of £4,077 for the 6,767 hectares (16,309 acres) and, if a freehold title were granted, it would have cost a further £600 to cover registration, stamp fees, and other formalities.

The agent put up a strong case for only one shilling an acre but asked the government for its ideas on the subject. The administration had apparently no ideas other than, possibly, Ross paying the costs of the proposed Mbulu-Oldeani-Ngorongoro road in the 1930–31 communications development plan.

Nowadays, the visitor to the Ngorongoro Crater may understandably be surprised at the amount of bickering over the comparatively small sums of money at stake in the controversy. It should be realized, however, that this all took place during a worldwide depression, and obviously money was worth so much more in those days, pound for pound.

Finally, at the end of 1932, when the minimum period of 25 years stipulated in Adolf Siedentopf's original leasehold title was up, the government had the opportunity to legally regain the farm as Crown land, providing that, 'in all fairness', Ross was compensated with the original purchase price of £4,600. The government was, however, unable to find sufficient funds for this compensation, and a suggestion that the Society for the Preservation of the Fauna of the Empire should raise this amount also met with no success.

No attempt to fence or alternatively develop the property was made, and so eventually, in 1939, under a new section of the Game Ordinance, the government succeeded in serving a notice on Sir Charles Ross's agent for his client to vacate the crater. It was not until 30 June 1940 that the lease was officially terminated and the farm became Crown land.

The mistake made by the administration after the First World War had taken two decades to remedy.

Various British secretaries of state for the colonies, governors, provincial commissioners, land agents, and an army of their minor officials had worked hard, but until then fruitlessly, to remedy the blunder. Tens of thousands of miles had been covered by commissions, committees, and individuals.

To be absolutely fair, the mistake made by the British government was inherited from that made by the German administration in 1907. It had, in fact, taken 33 years to solve the problem, and establish the framework of the unsurpassed game preservation area that the Ngorongoro Crater is today.

*A cheetah family, alert and watchful. The cubs will stay with their mother for up to two years, by which time they are adept hunters themselves.*

*The silver-backed jackal, a stealthy and adaptable predator and scavenger.*

*Two male Thomson's gazelles face off in a battle for territory.*

*A pair of zebra seek refreshment in the waters of Ngorongoro's Lake Magadi.*

# The Animals

The big attraction of the Ngorongoro Crater has always been the game population, and various discoveries would indicate that humans have lived in the area for millions of years. Neolithic man, whose graves have been excavated at the northern end of the crater next to the old Siedentopf farm, was a pastoralist and hunter. Like Adolf Siedentopf, he would have chosen this site for his living quarters due to a permanent water source from the Munge River. Furthermore, some 56 kilometres (35 miles) away is the Olduvai Gorge, where Mary Leakey found the 1.75-million-year-old *Australopithecus*. After her husband's death in 1972 she continued with her research in the area, resulting in the discovery of fossil hominid tracks at Laetoli dating back some 3.5 million years.

Evidence of prehistoric and strange-looking animals that were hunted by these civilizations was originally established in Olduvai by Kattwinkel and then again by Hans Reck prior to the First World War. Hans Reck excavated at Olduvai for three months in 1911, and in the 1,700 boxes he dispatched back to Berlin were some extraordinary finds. These included bones from 12 different mammoths, one complete but for the leg bones, which were too heavy to carry; *Deinotherium*, an extinct elephant with its tusks set in the lower jaw and curving downwards; *Pelorovis*, a gigantic animal related to either cattle or sheep with horns that spanned over 2 metres (6.5 feet); *Libytherium*, a massive giraffe with large sweeping horns; *Bularchus*, an immense pig with tusks nearly a metre (3 feet) long; and a hippo with eyes on the top of its head. It is interesting to observe that these various species have developed over millions of years to their modern-day equivalents, and most of them have retained their distinct characteristics.

Dr Baumann, who was the crater's first European visitor in 1892, compiled the first recorded history of game in the Ngorongoro Crater. He wrote: 'The abundance of game there was really magnificent: large herds of antelopes, together with long-maned gnus [wildebeest] and light-footed zebra.' He wrote also of the abundance of rhino and lion. A few years later, at the turn of the century, when the Siedentopf brothers had established their farms there, they found excessive numbers of game an endless problem. Various circumstances made farming in a high-density game area a nightmare. For example, during the calving season the wildebeest infected the cattle with *snotsiekte*, a form of fatal pleuropneumonia; and lions hunted after game which then demolished stockades and fences in an attempt to escape.

Prior to the First World War Adolf estimated that there were some 20,000 wildebeest, 1,500 zebra, several thousand hartebeest, Grant's gazelles, and Thomson's gazelles, an abundance of lion, leopard, and a few rhino. The Siedentopfs endeavoured to keep the game out of their half of the crater, but this was an almost impossible task. In an attempt to control the vast numbers they organized hunts, and one of the hunting guests recorded that the Siedentopf's staff, using ropes, drove about 8,000 wildebeest towards the hunters'

guns. Surprisingly, according to Adolf, these drastic measures appeared to make very little difference to their numbers. Following the evacuation of the Siedentopfs and their livestock from the crater during the First World War, there were a number of hunters, authors, and tourists whose estimates of game were, in most cases, greatly exaggerated.

The next recorded evaluation of game there was by the author and naturalist Andrew Pienaar ('Sangiro') in 1924. He recorded 60,000 wildebeest, zebra in 'noticeable herds', many hyena, small herds of Grant's and Thomson's gazelles, a few scattered hartebeest, many rhino, hippo, and elephant.

Five years later another author, F Radcliffe Holmes, estimated there to be 100,000 animals on the crater floor – undoubtedly a gross exaggeration. Not to be outdone, a few years later Lindgens wrote: 'In the middle of the bottom of the crater is situated a lake that contains water the whole year, the soda lake. Around the lake there are green plains with several hundred thousand head of game.'

Subsequently various game wardens and individuals who were actively associated with the future of the Ngorongoro put in their reports on the game population there. Even as recently as 1959 hunters M Behr and H O Meissner wrote of the crater: 'The many hundreds and often thousands of elephants and rhinos reassure every friend of the animals who has feared for the game of Africa.' If only, in retrospect, this had been true! Professor Bernhard Grzimek, director of Frankfurt Zoo, together with his son Michael, made the first really accurate census, by air, in 1958. They had previously made a film in Tanganyika called *No Room for Wild Animals*, which was a great success. Professor Grzimek then told Lieutenant Colonel Peter Molloy, director of national parks, that he intended to use the profit made from the film to buy private game land in Tanganyika, thus adding to the existing nature reserves in the country.

Molloy suggested that the money would be better spent on a detailed air survey of the seasonal migrations and populations of animals on the Serengeti plains and in the Ngorongoro Crater. At that time the very future of both the Serengeti and the crater were at stake, as will be seen in the next chapter. If they were to be saved it was vitally important to obtain considerably more accurate information than the several, often completely inaccurate surveys made in the past.

There were only three years to go before Tanganyika would have its *uhuru* (independence), and there was still the ongoing problem and conflicting interests of the Maasai resident at the southern end of the crater, the seasonal influx of fellow Maasai from outside, and the resident game. The British administration was determined to resolve these problems before independence, and attempted to establish a fair and effective compromise that would be equitable to both the Maasai and the wildlife. A steadily increasing influx of tourists over previous years had resulted in worldwide interest in the

*The migration of vast numbers of wildebeest and other herbivores through the Serengeti-Ngorongoro ecosystem is one of nature's most impressive spectacles.*

Ngorongoro and Serengeti. It was therefore vitally important to obtain more information on the ecosystem that existed there. An inadequate study of the climate, vegetation, and soil had been made, the area had yet to be mapped thoroughly, and the information of the migratory habits of the animals each year was insufficient. Here was an excellent opportunity for a detailed survey that would be completed by a distinguished and well-known wildlife conservationist and, furthermore, the Grzimeks would carry out this very expensive project at their own expense – it was an opportunity too good to be lost, and was accepted by the British government with open arms!

The Grzimeks bought a purpose-built Fiesler Stork light aircraft in Germany, successfully completed flying courses, and took off for Tanganyika to commence their task. Their very successful game survey of the Ngorongoro Crater and the Serengeti resulted in the publication of two books, *A Study of the Game of the Serengeti Plains* and *Serengeti Shall Not Die*, the latter being used later as the basis for an award-winning film.

This accurate aerial census revealed the following figures for the game population of the crater: 5,360 wildebeest, 1,767 zebra, 1,130 gazelle (Thomson's and Grant's), 112 elands, 19 rhinos, and 46 elephants – a total of some 8,500 animals.

Tragically, Michael was killed when the survey was almost completed, after his aircraft hit a vulture and crashed in the Serengeti on 10 January 1959. The memorial to him and his father, the late Professor Grzimek, is to be found at the side of the crater rim road, where they were buried.

A year later, national parks warden Gordon Harvey, accompanied by Molloy, made a follow-up survey of the area, and estimated the total count at 10,000, showing an increase of 1,500, mainly wildebeest.

Recent surveys indicate a resident population of some 20–25,000 animals, which is an increase of more than 100% in less than 40 years. As yet the Ngorongoro has not suffered unduly from this marked increase in animals, as there has also been a proportionate increase in predators, but it remains to be seen what will happen if this trend continues. Normally, when left to its own devices, nature provides its own balance and checks.

Although totalling only some 310 square kilometres (120 square miles), the floor of the crater has a fantastic variety of habitat: short- and long-grassed plains, temperate evergreen forest, gullies of lush gallery forest, swamps, lakes, and rivers.

There is a greater number and variety of wildlife species in the Ngorongoro Crater than in any other similar-sized area in Africa, and each habitat also has its own selection of bird varieties, both resident and migratory. With an estimated 500 species, the Ngorongoro is recognized as a birdwatcher's paradise.

Wildebeest, zebra, buffalo, warthog, Coke's hartebeest (kongoni), Thomson's gazelle, and Grant's gazelle graze on the open grassland, along with rhino, eland, and ostriches. If you are

*A few cheetah can be found in the vicinity of the Lerai Forest.*

*Best foot forward: Thomson's gazelles perform an elegant dance in flight.*

lucky, you will see one of the several cheetahs near the swamps or Lerai Forest. Five cheetahs were recorded in the September 1998 dry season game count. The rare mountain or Chandler's reedbuck and the diminutive dik-dik may be spotted on the steep inner slopes.

It is of particular interest to study the variety of animals in the crater and the changes that have taken place over the period of the past century.

Up to the First World War there were several thousand hartebeest. Since Siedentopf and Pienaar's observations of 'thousands' nobody has recorded more than a few dozen. Why did the hartebeest move out and back to the Serengeti? It could hardly be due to an influx of humans into the crater, as there must have been considerable disturbance, including the firing of many shots, when the Siedentopfs were having their periodic skirmishes with the wildebeest, and they also shared the grazing with 2,500 head of Maasai livestock. There is a possibility that they disliked the change of grazing when the Siedentopfs replaced the indigenous grasses with clover. The clover spread rapidly throughout the crater floor and is there to the present day.

It is also interesting that no buffalo were recorded in the Ngorongoro prior to 1960. From then onwards small herds of bachelor bulls became resident there, particularly after the eviction of the resident Maasai in 1974. Their numbers built up gradually as the cows started moving in, and by 1987 there were approximately 3,000, which had increased to 5,000 during the 1992 rains. An all-time high of 9,000 was recorded in 1999.

It is possible that the buffalo only started entering the crater to use it as a refuge after their numbers were decimated by a rinderpest epidemic in 1958 that also affected the wildebeest and eland. The inoculation of cattle bordering the Serengeti and the crater eradicated the disease by the 1960s, and since then the only outbreak was in 1982, affecting buffalo, eland, and giraffe, but not cattle.

The effect of the rinderpest epidemic was noticed at the internationally famous safari lodge, Gibb's Farm, which is next to my old coffee farm in Karatu. It adjoins the Ngorongoro and the Northern Highlands Forest Reserve (NHFR), and there is a path that the tourists use to walk through the forest to a waterfall. The larger animals originally used this old game trail, and they kept it cleared sufficiently for use by humans. When rinderpest started spreading, the visitors and their game guard often came across the sad sight of dead buffalo on or near the path. Since then, with the path no longer being used by larger animals, it did not take long for it to gradually become overgrown by stinging nettles and weeds, and now it must be cleared by hand.

During a three-year survey between 1990 and 1992 it was established that the buffalo population in the crater, with an average of approximately 3,000, consumed more grass annually than the 8,000 wildebeest present at the time. Statistics show that during the years 1963 to 1990, as the buffalo population increased, there was a decided and corresponding reduction in wildebeest. There are far too many buffalo now resident on the crater floor for the lion and hyena to handle, and, in any case, they tend to prefer wildebeest and zebra, which are much easier to kill.

Added to the increase in population of the other game species over recent years, the buffalo herds there may well soon present a dilemma. It is impossible to drive the buffalo out of the crater, and the only way to reduce their numbers before they destroy their and other species' habitat would be to cull them. Should this prove to be the only answer, international animal lovers would be up in arms and unable to understand this as a 'final solution'. There are so many buffalo that it would be an impossible task to drug them and move them out – and even if it were feasible, they would probably return soon afterwards.

Fortunately the balance of nature invariably works in its own way, and it will be interesting to observe what happens over the next decade – maybe the buffalo themselves will find a solution.

The Ngorongoro elephant have always been renowned for their body size and the weight of their ivory – at the conservation office there is a pair of tusks weighing over 60 kilograms (130 pounds) each. Before the First World War the German and South African hunters targeted this area for big 'tuskers'.

There are always at least 70 bull elephant which enter and leave the crater from the adjacent forest reserve. Abundant water and browse, together with ample salt licks, ensure that the NHFR, a vital section of the Ngorongoro Conservation Area (NCA), will continue to be a favourite locality for elephant. Breeding herds of cows and calves, however, shun the crater floor, most probably because they realize there is insufficient food for them there.

Elephants were continually invading all our farms along the borders of the conservation area in Oldeani and Karatu and, although poaching in the 1970s and 1980s considerably reduced their numbers, they still occasionally raid these farms. The professional hunting ban, enforced in 1973, resulted in almost uncontrollable, massive poaching of rhino and elephant throughout Tanzania. One of the main curbs on poaching had been the policing of the remote, game-filled areas by professional hunters operating licensed, legitimate hunting safaris, accompanied by government Game Department game guards. Once the professional safaris were out of the way, the poachers ran amok, and even resorted to using helicopters in the most remote elephant strongholds, like the Selous Game Reserve in southern Tanzania. When the hunting ban was lifted in 1979, the professional hunting safaris once more assisted tremendously in curbing poaching activities.

Unfortunately, all too frequently there was, and still is, an ongoing battle between

*A dramatic confrontation between rhino and buffalo. The bulkier rhino will be almost twice the weight of its adversary.*

*A leopard lazes in the fork of a tree, safe from more earthbound antagonists such as lion.*

'visiting' game and the farmers adjoining the NCA at Oldeani, Karatu, Mbulumbulu, and elsewhere. The most destructive of these visitors are the elephant and buffalo. A herd of buffalo or elephant can devastate acres of maize, wheat, or beans in a few hours, and game guards from the Ngorongoro Conservation Area Authority (NCAA) have to periodically shoot out game to protect farmers and their crops.

The nearest large bodies of water to the Ngorongoro where hippo are prevalent are lakes Eyasi and Manyara, both about 50 kilometres (30 miles) away in mountainous county, and the first hippo to move onto the crater floor would have had to travel from either of these two lakes. The ability of hippo to instinctively travel long distances to reach alternative water has often been recorded in various parts of Africa. This was, tragically, proven to me in 1979 in Zambia. The rains had been very poor that year, and the spring water at my campsite, which had been present for three previous years, had dried up. Every second day my staff had to collect water from a large waterhole a few miles from camp. Sadly, one of the porters was fatally attacked by a bull hippo whilst he was filling a water drum – there had never been hippo at that pool before, and the nearest water in which I had seen hippo was over 50 kilometres (30 miles) away!

One of the unexplained phenomena of the wildlife population on the crater floor is the absence of warthog until 1976. Since then, numbers have averaged between 50 and 100, with a high of 336 recorded in 1988.

Interestingly, the local Maasai claim many of their old shields are made from the hide of the rare giant forest hog. Colonel Meinertzhagen introduced the giant forest hog to the lists of African game species after a hunting safari in 1904. The first reported sighting at the Ngorongoro Crater was in 1921, when a specimen taken at Matjekgesberge was declared a subspecies *Hylochoerus meinertzhageni schultzi*. The Kenya wildlife magazine, *Africana*, recorded in 1971 that 'at 12 p.m. on Sept 20, 1970, 4 miles west of Wogakuria, a large giant forest hog was seen 150 yards from the track, in open country. This is the first record of the species for Serengeti and only the second for all Tanzania. Giant forest hog have occasionally been recorded from the Kenya Maasai Mara country, 40 miles to the north-west.' T A Barns states in his book *Across the Great Craterland to the Congo* that he saw giant forest hog in the forest glades on the eastern crater rim track. More recently, in 1968, Per and Margaret Kullender of Gibb's Farm also sighted one on the same track. It is extremely probable that this rare game species has survived in the densest forest of the NHFR near the crater.

There has always been a large population of resident lion in the crater, including a number of magnificent black-maned specimens. In 1962, however, the lion population dropped to 15 following a plague of biting flies. Their numbers built up rapidly afterwards and a tourist visiting the Ngorongoro would have to be extremely unlucky not to spot lion feeding on a kill of (most likely) wildebeest or zebra, or lying satiated near the carcass. Together with more than 400 hyena which inhabit the crater floor, the lions prey on the sick, lame, and dying and ensure that only the fittest specimens survive. During the late 1960s, filming at night using special lenses, it was established that hyenas, in fact, were making at least half of the 'lion kills' on the crater floor. Once the hyenas had a successful kill they often made so much noise about it that they attracted the lions, who were only too pleased to drive them off and accept an easily acquired meal! Nowadays the lions make most of their own kills.

The predators' final tidying up is carried out by vultures, marabou storks, and all three types of jackal – the silver-backed, golden, and the rare side-striped.

There are very few leopards on the crater floor, usually lurking mostly around the Munge River area. They are very secretive and are seldom seen. The surrounding NHFR, however, has a large population of leopards. They feed mainly on bushbuck, reedbuck, dik-dik, and other smaller game. These leopards have adapted themselves to the altitude and low temperatures of the forest reserve, and are renowned for their beautiful pelts. To combat the cold they have a longer, thicker fur, old ivory in colour with jet-black rosettes, and the males are generally bigger than those on the crater floor or at lesser altitudes.

It has been recorded throughout Africa, including in the NHFR, that, by preference, when available, leopards prefer domestic dog meat to game. During the 17 years I farmed next to the Ngorongoro on Shangri-La estate I averaged a loss of three to four dogs a year to the leopards that wandered down from the forest reserve. These leopards were all males and measured more than 2.1 metres (7 feet) from the tip of the tail to the nose.

Amazingly, over that period, never, on a single occasion, was I on the farm when my dogs were attacked as, uncannily, the leopards always seemed to sense when I would be away, even if only for a day or so. I would return to find at least one of my pack of large dogs had been killed and eaten. My labour force of over 100 had many young children and there were also hundreds of goats and immature cattle, all at risk from marauding leopard. Unfortunately it was always necessary to either catch, where possible, or kill the unwelcome intruder.

Some of the species present in the Serengeti choose not to enter the crater. These include topi and impala, apparently due to their preference for the acacia woodland area. Lack of browse, understandably, rules out the presence of giraffe, although large numbers are present on the north-west, reverse wall of the crater where their favourite acacia abounds.

Sadly, the only game species there that has suffered tremendously over the past 30 years, almost to the point of extinction, is the black rhino. Their position started deteriorating directly after Tanganyika National Parks handed over the jurisdiction of the crater area to the newly formed NCAA on 1 July 1959. At the time I was still farming at

*Wildebeest find grazing on the shores of Lake Magadi.*

Karatu, and the reports leaking back to me of the slaughter of rhino at the Ngorongoro were so disturbing I made a special trip there with Bernard Kunicki, a professional photographer from Kenya. Our visit resulted in an article published in the national newspaper, the *Tanganyika Standard*, on 5 November 1959.

I stressed that large numbers of Maasai, herding about 25,000 head of stock, had moved into the NCA from the Moru Kopjes – the game migratory corridor which was exchanged by the National Parks for the Ngorongoro, as detailed in the next chapter.

I wrote: 'The Maasai probably felt they had achieved a major victory when the Parks left.' They had killed six rhino. 'The actions of a small number of young Maasai in spearing six rhino must on no account be interpreted as typical of the attitude of the Maasai to game in the crater … There is no doubt whatsoever that the great majority of the older Maasai deplore the deaths of the six rhino. Many have actively assisted in bringing the culprits to justice.' I made the significant point, however, that the horns had been removed from only two of the carcasses, which would indicate alternative reasons for their deaths than the recovery of the horns.

I added: 'Since rhino hunting was banned in Tanganyika earlier this year rhino horn prices have risen sky high.' Like everything in life, once removed from being readily available, the price rises.

My article concluded: 'The game in the crater is not being wiped out. It is still one of the finest game sanctuaries in Africa and there is every indication that it will remain so.'

The Tanganyika government sent overseas several thousand copies of this article to allay international fears for the future of the crater, and titled it 'The Truth About the Ngorongoro'.

Sadly, however, the rhino position continued to deteriorate.

I wrote a sequel to my article upon my return to the crater a year later following further alarming reports on the situation there. This was printed in the *Tanganyika Standard* on 20 November 1960, and was titled 'Wanton Slaughter of Rhino – their days are numbered unless drastic action is taken'. It stated that at least another 20 rhino had been killed during this period, and that a minimum of 54 rhino had been killed in the NCA. Undoubtedly, other rhino would have been killed in more inaccessible spots and the carcasses not yet found. More than half of the rhino killed had had their horns removed, and investigation had shown that some of the local moran were being used as professional rhino hunters by visiting traders from a non-Tanganyikan tribe. They were being paid either in cash or in kind – generally, illegal drugs. It is probable that other rhino had been killed by the moran purely from

*A black rhino, still clinging on as a resident of the Ngorongoro despite being poached almost to extinction over the decades.*

*A hyena eyes up a rhino calf as a potential meal, but its mother may have other ideas.*

bravado to impress their girlfriends and fellow moran with their 'courage'. When taken to court, however, some escaped punishment with the plea of self-defence! Where there had been a self-defence plea, the rhino had been speared behind the shoulder, and it is quite obvious to anyone who has ever been charged by a rhino, or been put in the position of having to defend himself from one, that under such circumstances a spear thrust in this position is virtually an impossibility.

My article went on to suggest various measures that might be used to control the slaughter.

Following the syndication of this article with the international press there was a worldwide reaction by wildlife conservationists, condemning the apparently uncontrollable and steady decimation of the rhino.

Well to the forefront of international recognition was Professor Grzimek, whose books, films, and lectures on the Ngorongoro Crater and the Serengeti had done so much to preserve the area. Shortly after he read the article on the slaughter of the rhino Grzimek, as a matter of urgency, visited the crater and wrote a very strong report on the results of his visit. Directly after his visit he received a cable from President Nyerere summoning him to Dar es Salaam, the capital of Tanganyika, to discuss the rhino situation. This discussion with the president resulted in an intensive 'Save the Rhino' campaign.

Although some rhino poaching continued in the area in spite of all the efforts being made to protect them, the rhino position was still positive when Canadian biologist John Goddard commenced a three-year study of the species in the crater and Olduvai Gorge in 1964. He established that there was a total of 108 rhino using the crater and 63 in the vicinity of Olduvai – a grand total of 171. I well remember querying these exact figures with John since, even at close range, many rhino appear to have identical horns. He showed me the photographs he had taken of each and every specimen, with the accompanying nickname he had given them. The characteristics used for identification of each individual were the size and shape of the anterior and posterior horns, peculiarities of the ears, and the contour pattern of wrinkles in the snout. Similarly to the fingerprints of humans, no two rhinos have identical wrinkles.

Regrettably, particularly in the 1970s, rhino and elephant poaching became almost totally uncontrollable throughout Tanzania. The political decision in 1977 to close the international border between Tanzania and Kenya resulted in a drastic increase in poaching activities in the Serengeti, overlapping into the NCA.

There was a staggering drop in foreign visitors to the Park from some 70,000 in 1976 to 10,000 in 1977. Foreign exchange from tourists continued to decline until 1986 when the border was partially reopened. The operating budget for the Serengeti

National Park subsidizes the cost of anti-poaching patrols. From 1982 to 1985 the budget dropped considerably, even showing a loss over several years up to 1987. Insufficient funds consequently resulted in a great reduction in anti-poaching activities to 60% of the operations prior to the border closure.

The ecosystems of the Serengeti and the NCA are so closely interwoven that the NCA also had poaching problems during this period. In 1981 I made another of my regular visits to the crater and found two freshly killed rhino carcasses there. Both rhino had been shot with large-calibre rifles, and the location was only 3.2 kilometres (2 miles) from one of the three game guard camps on the floor of the crater. I once again felt it necessary to put pen to paper, and another article was published in the *Tanzania Standard* in June 1981, resulting in worldwide condemnation.

Today there are less than 20 rhino left in the Ngorongoro and only a few left in inaccessible areas around the country. Every effort is being made to protect these survivors through round-the-clock surveillance.

*Each rhino can be identified by its unique horn and wrinkle characteristics.*

*A confrontation between two black rhinos.*

*Concerned adults nuzzle a newborn wildebeest foal to its feet. Its survival depends on its ability to move immediately with the herd.*

*In contrast to herbivore offspring, hyena cubs are completely helpless at birth.*

*Heads down: zebra and flamingo indulge in their separate dietary preferences.*

*A lioness gingerly carries her cub to a safe haven.*

# The Ngorongoro as a Legislated Game Sanctuary

As we have seen, prior to the First World War the German government wanted to establish the whole of the crater as a game sanctuary but Adolf Siedentopf's legal residence there on Farm Soltau had effectively stymied this move. One of the few measures of game control in place there was the prohibition on shooting rhino.

After the war the same plans were again handicapped by the unfortunate sale of Adolf's farm to Sir Charles Ross, and the leasing of his brother's farm to Harry Hurst. If it had not been for the outbreak of war in 1914, the crater area would have been further alienated for farming and hunting concessions. In spite of this, the British administration legislated several times to preserve and conserve the game of the Ngorongoro and the Serengeti, pending the eviction of Ross.

Since the numbers of large animals in the crater are associated with the movements and migrations of game in the Serengeti, it is impossible to divorce the two areas. Therefore this chapter is devoted to the continuity of legislation for both areas from directly after the First World War up to the present day.

In 1921, during Ross's lease of Soltau, Britain, as the mandatory power of Tanganyika for the League of Nations, enacted the first Game Preservation Ordinance. Provision was made for the institution of three categories of game reserve: 'partial', 'complete', and 'closed'.

From reading through the text it would appear that the intention was to make a closed reserve the highest form of protected area, as power was given to the governor to order the control and regulation of human entry and activities within its boundaries. However, on closer inspection of the various game regulations enacted in the ordinance, it becomes evident that, in practice, a complete reserve was more sacrosanct than a closed one. The provision within the Game Preservation Ordinance relating to hunting and human activities in reserves was made 'subject to anything otherwise prescribed by regulation'. Thus, up to the repeal of the ordinance in 1940, hunting of any species was forbidden in a complete reserve, but possible in a closed reserve with a provincial commissioner's permit.

During 1928 the Ngorongoro Crater, with its boundaries formed by the rim, but excluding Soltau, became a complete reserve. All hunting there was thus prohibited, subject to some strictly limited exceptions.

A year later an area in the western Serengeti was also declared a complete game reserve, and this then became the Serengeti closed reserve in 1930. The perimeter ran from Lake Victoria to a line somewhat loosely defined that lay a little to the left of Seronera, and south to a place on the Mbalangeti River. It was specifically stated that the only restriction of human activity within this area was in respect of hunting and photography. This suggests that other restrictions on human entry and their use of land within the area were not lawfully prescribed by regulations due to the impracticability of enforcing them. Considering the enormous area involved this is not surprising.

Both the crater and the western half of the existing present-day Serengeti National Park were recognized as two vital wildlife areas and, accordingly, given the highest protection as regards to hunting during the years 1930 to 1940 – at least on paper!

A vast area outside these focal points, comprising what would become the limits of the Serengeti National Park in 1957, together with much land to the north of it, was recognized as requiring varying degrees of protection. By 1937 this degree of protection amounted to a complete prohibition of hunting of the following species within the Serengeti closed reserve: lion, cheetah, leopard, giraffe, rhinoceros, buffalo, roan antelope, hyena, and wild dog.

During the 1930s American film companies began to realize that their filmgoers were greatly interested in Africa's wild game. Hollywood scriptwriters vied with one another to include the most spectacular shots of big game in their scripts. Provided they did not disturb the game too much with their activities, they were encouraged by the Game Department and consequently brought in an influx of badly needed dollars. Due to the vastness of the Serengeti complete reserve there was obviously only a limited amount of control possible with just one game warden and a few game askaris.

The activities of these overseas visitors resulted in some quite extraordinary situations that fortunately, and surprisingly, occurred without loss of life.

One film company concentrated on the famous Serengeti lions for their more spectacular shots. They 'tamed' one large pride of lions by providing their food. This was done by initially dragging a game carcass behind one of their camera cars to within a short distance of the lions; the bait was then cast off and the eating of the carcass could be filmed. The lions were fed daily and, as they became progressively less shy, they followed the 'meat wagon' and tried to feed on the carcass whilst it was being dragged. When they became really tame, the rope was shortened until their meal was directly next to the safari car, which had an open-sided roof.

The next development was to place the carcass on top of the car, and spectacular footage was filmed from another vehicle of the lions leaping onto the top of their 'larder'. By smearing the roof of the safari car with game blood and meat scent but without supplying the usual ration of meat to the lions, the film unit eventually had the pride consistently jumping onto the roof of the car! This was all very well while it lasted, for both the film script and the lions, but after the unit returned to Hollywood ordinary game viewers, quietly driving their vehicles through the same area, had the horrifying experience of being 'attacked' as the same pride of lions leapt onto the car roof, looking for the customary meat ration!

*Flamingo flocks constitute the largest biomass of birds per hectare on the planet.*

*The rich grasslands of the Ngorongoro support vast herds of grazing animals.*

*A film crew familiarizes a pride of lions with their roles (page 120).*

*Lions and actors share their dining space (this page).*

Another film unit went to even more extreme and dangerous lengths to provide their audience with greater thrills by using the Serengeti lions. They started with the same technique of 'taming' a lion pride by dragging game carcasses, but then enticed them to come into the safari camp where the meat was then released! The terrified actors were seated at a dining table next to the lions, which were busy enjoying their handout, and the equally terrified African staff served the various courses. The final spectacular shot showed the actors eating their food with, in the same frame, the lions having their lunch!

The frightening experience of subsequent visitors pitching camp in the same area can easily be imagined!

The next legislative landmark in the history of the Serengeti National Park was the enactment of Game Ordinance 1940 (Cap. 159). As the preamble indicated, the purpose of this ordinance was to give effect to the provisions of the Convention Relative to the Preservation of Fauna and Flora in Their Natural State, signed in London on 8 November 1933, of which the Tanganyika government was a signatory.

This convention, although it did not bind the contracting states too rigorously, had recognized that the preservation of natural fauna and flora was an international responsibility. The convention felt that the best way of ensuring preservation was the creation within national territories of areas known as 'national parks'. These denoted areas which, once the boundaries had been fixed, could not be altered or alienated, except by competent legislative authority.

It is perhaps worth noting, in the light of subsequent history, that this convention was vague with respect to the degree of human activity permissible within a national park. The contracting parties merely promised to consider how far human settlements within national park limits could be controlled, with a view to ensuring that the natural fauna and flora had the minimum disturbance.

The same article stipulated that the hunting, killing, or capturing of fauna, and the destruction of flora in a park, should be prohibited except by, or under the direction or control of, the park authorities.

The Game Ordinance delimited and designated an area as the Serengeti National Park. This included the complete reserve of the western Serengeti, the Ngorongoro Crater, and a proportion of the Serengeti closed reserve. It is interesting to note that the south-western side of the park included the headwaters of the Simiyu and Dumma rivers and, on its southern side, a portion of the Endulen area. As will be seen later, these areas were lost to the park when the first national park administered by trustees was created in 1951.

The portions not included ceased to be reserves, but became protected areas under the provisions of Section 4, and the hunting of all carnivore and some species of herbivore was prohibited. Elephant, zebra, and wildebeest could be hunted only on a game warden's or provincial commissioner's permit. Within the park area the hunting of any animals was prohibited except on a governor's permit.

It is important to note that this ordinance, for the first time, tried to restrict entry into a park, and allowed only very limited hunting there. Entry into or residence within the park was declared unlawful except on special permit. This concerned the people whose place of birth or ordinary residence was within the park, such as the Maasai and Wanderobo, and those who had any rights over immovable property, such as Asian storekeepers. The governor-in-council was empowered to make regulations that controlled settlements in national parks in order to prevent disturbance to the natural fauna.

It is also interesting to note that this ordinance contained a provision which, when strictly interpreted, meant that the lighting of a bush or grass fire, wilfully or negligently, within the park area was made a criminal offence. It became obvious that this section proved unenforceable after a survey of the park by Professor Pearsall in 1956. His report was to prove the keystone of the future of the Serengeti and the Ngorongoro.

To sum up the effect of the 1940 ordinance: whilst the ordinance recognized the principle of a national park it introduced no great change in the degree of control exercised over the area. The administration remained the responsibility of government, advised by the Game Department. There is no evidence that the tribes accustomed to using the area for grazing or residence were in any way restricted. Here the position rested during the period of the Second World War, when the government was absorbed with other issues.

The revival of interest in game preservation after the war resulted in the enactment of a further National Parks Ordinance in 1948, but this was not enforced until 1951 owing to difficulties in the fixing of boundaries. It repealed many sections of the previous Game Ordinance and established the principle of national parks being administered by a board of trustees. Once the boundaries were established the Serengeti National Park was proclaimed in 1951.

The responsibility for controlling and managing any area declared a national park lay with a board of trustees, who were given powers to appoint a board of management. The composition of the board indicated that government and the legislature fully recognized the importance of national parks and the wide interest shown in their development, both locally and internationally. Therefore, in addition to government nominees and commercial representatives, provision was made for the appointment of honorary trustees, who would be persons of eminence in scientific or other fields. The late Professor Grzimek came into this category.

The ordinance conferred certain powers of arrest on authorized trustee representatives, and stipulated that anyone arrested by a park official had to be brought before a magistrate

and, if convicted, would be liable to a fine and/or imprisonment for up to two years. These were drastic measures designed for the suppression of poaching and other destructive abuses. In 1957 the Serengeti Committee observed that, as this applied to an area ordinarily free of human settlement, there would have been no embarrassment, save to a wrongdoer. The committee recommended that no national park should include an area where it was impracticable or impossible for government to exclude human residence and land use.

The administration and trustees prepared proposals which had as their main objective the establishment of a true national park, entirely free from human interest in all the more important areas within the (then) park boundaries. It was realized that this could only be achieved if the Maasai could be persuaded to relinquish the rights that they could lawfully claim in those areas, and this would require some inducement.

It was therefore proposed that in the remaining areas of the existing park the Maasai should be allowed to continue to follow, or modify, their traditional way of life, subject only to close control of hunting. The Maasai were approached and accepted the proposals, in principle.

The government then took further steps to ensure that the Maasai fully understood the implications of the proposals, and also, by examination on the ground, to ensure that there would be no further misunderstanding about proposed boundaries. The outcome of these investigations and negotiations was less favourable to the trustees than their original proposals. The Maasai proved obdurate in their requirements, and the only boundaries to which they would agree fell short of what the trustees had represented as their minimum requirements.

The government, however, was satisfied that the Maasai had gone as far as they could reasonably be expected to go, and that it would be 'neither wise nor proper' to press them further, since the boundary question was the key to the successful conclusion of the negotiations. Proposals on what the Maasai were willing to concede were then formally submitted to the trustees, who accepted them reluctantly, and made them subject to a number of provisos which were accepted by the government.

The proposals were that the Serengeti National Park should be modified to constitute three national parks, free from all human rights. These areas were the Ngorongoro area (1,150 square kilometres/450 square miles), the Empakaai Crater near the Ngorongoro (26 square kilometres/10 square miles), and the western Serengeti area (3,600 square kilometres/1,400 square miles), in Lake Province.

It was further proposed that the great central Serengeti plains, extending some 6,700 square kilometres (2,600 square miles) and covering the larger part of the area to be removed from the existing national park, should be protected by special legislation. This legislation, while providing free right of access by the Maasai and their domestic livestock

*A spotted hyena rests in the midday sun.*

for seasonal grazing, would prevent development in the area that might interfere with the normal migration and seasonal grazing of game, or be in any way inimical to game.

The areas bordering the new parks, one to the north of the Ngorongoro Crater and including most of the balance of the Crater Highlands, and the other based on the Moru Kopjes, were to become development areas. It was proposed that these areas, under improved pasturage and permanent water supplies, would replace the Ngorongoro for Maasai cattle husbandry, and would be freed from any special restrictions, with the interests of game generally subordinate to those of man.

In addition, the principal boundary between the Lake and (then) Northern provinces, cutting through the centre of the plains, should be moved westwards to bring the Maasai, hitherto resident in Lake Province, within the area of jurisdiction of the Maasai Native Authority.

Three further extensions to the existing national park were proposed for three other areas in Lake Province.

These, in broad outline, were the main proposals included in the sessional paper. Few people, including the trustees, the Maasai, and the government, realized how the paper would boomerang, bringing in interested parties throughout the world, and causing a furore of indignation and controversy.

There followed a positive avalanche of important memoranda, which undoubtedly influenced and guided the 1957 Serengeti Commission of Enquiry. These memoranda covered every possible factor concerning the past, present, and future of game; the Maasai; grazing; water resources; stock diseases; tribal tradition; and all other material relevant to the reconstitution of the Serengeti National Park and the Ngorongoro.

The most important of them all was the 'Report on an Ecological Survey of the Serengeti National Park, Tanganyika', by Professor W H Pearsall, D.Sc., FRS, of the University of London. The report gave incontestable facts on the ecology of the area and served as a base for all later deliberations of the commission on the future of the park.

Other important memoranda included 'Fauna of the Serengeti National Park', prepared by the chief game warden, G H Swynnerton; and memoranda prepared by the Maasai, the board of trustees, the Wildlife Societies of Kenya and Tanganyika, and the American Committee for International Wildlife Protection. This was the most crucial stage of the recent history of the Serengeti and the Ngorongoro Crater.

When the government realized that the future of these areas had become a world issue they set up the Serengeti Commission of Enquiry in 1957 under the chairmanship of Sir Barclay Nihill, KBE, MC, who was formerly the president of the Court of Appeal for Eastern Africa.

The objective deliberations of the commission are best summed up by the following paragraph in their report: 'National parks are international assets and we believe they should be secured, as far as possible, against frequent changes of policy or of personalities in government, and we appreciate that to achieve this objective our deliberations must be based not only on scientific desirability but on general equity in the widest sense of the word.'

The commission rolled up its sleeves and got down to work. They held many private and public sessions, met and heard the viewpoints of every section of the community, studied many memoranda, and visited the Serengeti and the crater, before publishing their excellent and far-sighted report on 7 August 1957.

The number of animals; grazing; damage by fire; cutting of trees; damage to water resources; poaching; and conflicts of interest were but representative of the many facets covered by the enquiry, and reported on by the committee, before making its final detailed recommendations.

The main aim or 'bottom line' was, of course, to find a lasting solution to the oft-repeated problem of resolving the conflict between the needs of the resident Maasai population and the preservation of the Serengeti National Park and the Ngorongoro Crater as unique and incomparable fauna and flora conservation areas.

'It seems clear that when the Serengeti National Park was first created, in 1940, under the Game Ordinance, little thought was given to the ultimate consequences of permitting the activities of pastoral people within its boundaries', the report stated.

Many of the memoranda submitted to the committee had drawn attention to the fact that areas proposed as national parks in the white paper bore no relation to the actual requirements of the wild animals throughout the cycle of their migrations, and that the problem called for a more scientific approach.

The white paper proposals for wildlife areas to be secondary to Maasai occupation were rejected. The committee had 'abundant evidence' that Moru was a key point in the movement of the wild animals, as well as being the chief source of water for the western Serengeti. There was also evidence of deterioration caused by the felling of trees and burning of vegetation, with consequent damage to permanent springs.

'We consider therefore that Moru is a locality which requires the highest conservation status to prevent deterioration to a condition in which it would be

*An ostrich strolls near Lake Magadi.*

worthless for any purpose; and that in view of its importance to the cycle of western migratory animals (to and from the Ngorongoro), human rights should be excluded from the area completely.'

The white paper proposal that the Ngorongoro should become one of the three 'true national parks' was also rejected.

The committee recommended that the first priority here should be the human inhabitant, and that game should be only a second priority, adequately protected. 'The highland forests are the main source of water in the whole of the existing park, and contain a large number of inhabitants. As such, these highlands must be conserved and developed to improve their natural resources for the use of man.'

They recommended a project 'of some magnitude' to conserve water supplies, forest, and pasture. The committee stressed, as a 'secondary consideration', the tourist attraction of the scenery and wildlife at the Ngorongoro Crater and the Empakaai Crater, and stated that they should be conserved for this purpose 'as far as is compatible with the main objective already stated'.

The remaining white paper proposal, that the great central plain should be removed from the national park, was also rejected, primarily on the grounds that alternate use in different seasons – by migratory game and Maasai cattle – would be destructive to grass cover, and would eventually endanger the habitat. It was stressed that this plain was the main wet season habitat of the plains game migrating from the west, and should be preserved, particularly since the area was of only marginal value for human use.

There were various other recommendations made by the committee, including the reconstitution of the national park in the western Serengeti; its extension northwards to include uninhabited territory and provide a link with the Maasai Mara National Reserve in Kenya; plus various boundary recommendations for both the western Serengeti and the Ngorongoro area. Practically all these recommendations were accepted and became law.

Since the committee rejected all the more important proposals in the white paper, one wonders whether the paper was intended purely as a 'cockshy'! If so, it certainly achieved the aim of obtaining more details from competent experts of the various factors concerning the park, before coming to a final decision on its future. Alternatively, the proposed reconstitution could well have been purely political expediency, to alleviate pressure from the Maasai. Certainly the committee's strong recommendations regarding the importance of the highlands led directly to the formation of the NCAA, which took over from National Parks on 1 July 1959.

*A group of wildebeest in flight.*

*The dense forest of the crater sides contrasts with the broad grasslands below.*

*Lush forests adorn the steep inner face of the crater.*

*Visitors to the Ngorongoro can generally find peaceful solitude in its wide vistas.*

*An unusually large flock of yellow-billed storks in majestic flight.*

*A young elephant enjoys a dust bath.*

# The Ngorongoro Conservation Area Authority

The Ngorongoro Conservation Area (NCA), covering 8,300 square kilometres (3,200 square miles), was the first protected area in Africa to be designated for a dynamic multiple land use system, perpetuating the historical balance of people and nature.

Emulated now worldwide, this system tackles the delicate balance of wildlife protection, supporting indigenous residents, protecting natural resources, and, at the same time, promoting and accommodating tourism. The NCA, together with the Serengeti National Park and other conservation areas of the Serengeti ecosystem, supports the greatest concentration of wildlife left on earth.

The short grass plains of the NCA are the wet season grazing grounds for the majority of the Serengeti migrating herds which now number, approximately, 1.5 million wildebeest, 470,000 gazelles, and 260,000 zebra, whilst the crater also supports the highest predator concentration in Africa. High densities of wildlife are supported in the crater throughout the year, and here is one of the last populations of black rhinoceros in the country.

Included in the NCA is the Northern Highlands Forest Reserve (NHFR). This is a vital water catchment area, providing water for use both within the NCA and for the adjacent subsistence and commercial agricultural communities of Oldeani and Karatu. Additional to its catchment value, the highland forest also provides important habitat for game, including rhinoceros, elephant, and buffalo.

As we have already seen, two of the most important archaeological and palaeontological sites in the world, Olduvai Gorge and Laetoli, are found within the NCA. The area contains many other palaeontological/archaeological sites, and the chance of further discoveries in the future is high.

Recognizing the importance of the NCA to mankind, the United Nations Educational, Scientific and Cultural Organization (UNESCO) has accorded it the status of a World Heritage Site and International Biosphere Reserve. Visitors are also attracted to these features and the area has become one of the most visited tourist destinations in Tanzania.

The NCA, however, is more than of purely biological and archaeological interest, and has been the traditional homeland for the Maasai for nearly two centuries. Evidence suggests that pastoralists in one form or another have existed here for some 2,000 years.

Multiple land use philosophy in the NCA aims to maintain the coexistence of pastoralists and wildlife in a natural, traditional setting. This philosophy is admirably suited here because the rich and varied resources allow utilization with little competition – given proper planning. Based on these facts, therefore, human development, conservation, and tourism are three components that are considered to be compatible in the area.

The delicate task of successfully balancing the often conflicting interests of wildlife and people, within the framework of interrelated natural resources, has not, however, been easy. Many other interdependent services and resources are involved in a complex infrastructure.

Wildlife management, forestry, water resources, veterinary and social services, education, health, archaeology, anti-poaching, and other associated factors are also involved.

As far back as 1975, 16 years after the birth of the NCA, the complex administrative problems of the multifaceted operation led to the inauguration of the Ngorongoro Conservation Area Authority (NCAA). This elevated the status of the NCA administrative body to an autonomous parastatal organization.

The purposes of the NCAA, as set out in the General Management Plan of 1997, are as follows:

- To maintain a dynamic multiple land use system which perpetuates the historical balance of people and nature
- To conserve the biodiversity and ecological integrity of the Serengeti ecosystem and the Ngorongoro Highlands
- To conserve the area's internationally significant palaeontological and archaeological sites and resources
- To protect water catchments vital to the region's ecology and residents
- To safeguard and promote the rights of indigenous residents of the area and to control their own economic and cultural development in a manner that leaves exceptional resources intact
- To encourage responsible tourism which benefits the local, regional, and national economy
- To provide opportunities for interpretation, research, and education concerning the area's natural and cultural resources
- To promote and maintain those values for which the area is designated a World Heritage Site and International Biosphere Reserve

The research and planning unit (RPU) of the NCA will play an increasingly important part in the present General Management Plan.

Most important is research to further identify and safeguard wildlife corridors and important habitats. The Serengeti and Salai plains in the NCA have already been safeguarded for the important role they have in the annual wildebeest migration in the Serengeti ecosystem. Other wildlife corridors and movements within the area, with the exception of the crater, require further considerable study. The plains in the area are also a primary calving area for migratory wildebeest.

Listed among the threatened animal species are black rhino, elephant, wild dog, and cheetah. At greatest risk is the rhino. As we have seen, poaching has drastically reduced the crater population of this species from over 100 in the 1960s to only 12 resident and

*The steep gradients of the fringing highlands generate clouds which produce copious rain, making this an important water catchment area.*

*A lion cub enjoys the comfort and security of its mother.*

transient rhino in 1995. Stepped-up anti-poaching measures are being implemented, and the dwindling rhino numbers there are the focus for continual monitoring and studies for their protection. Existing ranger posts will be increased and upgraded with qualified personnel, firearms, and equipment. The anti-poaching unit, which is the primary reaction force for anti-poaching, will provide full-time surveillance and protection of the rhino population in the crater. A third force, a scout unit, will be a mobile unit, providing foot patrols and monitoring wildlife.

Inbreeding in the small rhino population requires urgent extra research into the threat of genetic isolation. In late 1995 there were only two adult rhino males and three adult females. Research results will almost certainly require the relocation of other rhinos and/or artificial insemination, providing there is no undue risk to the species.

The lion population in the Ngorongoro Crater shows a lack of genetic diversity and is suspected to have genetic abnormalities as a result of inbreeding. Continued research into genetic isolation of the lion population and its potential effects will therefore be encouraged by the RPU.

The following is a summary of the proposed actions of the RPU:

- Continue intensive monitoring of black rhinoceros; support research on species for which there is insufficient information, particularly giant forest hog, lammergeier, and pancake tortoise
- Support further research into genetic isolation and inbreeding of black rhino and lion, and take appropriate action as identified by research
- Upgrade the existing ranger posts system
- Establish an anti-poaching scout unit made up largely of indigenous residents
- Maintain the anti-poaching unit at the Olduvai Gorge and improve training and equipment
- Support research on threatened plant species
- Improve conservation, education, and community conservation activities for residents concerning rhino, elephant, and other threatened species
- Strengthen the Livestock Department of the Community Development Department of the NCA, providing wildlife veterinary services to control disease outbreaks

The last priority is most important. As we have seen, cattle have always been the basis of the Maasai economy and their food security, but cattle numbers have declined drastically since 1960, when it was established that they numbered 160,000. Their numbers had dropped to 100,000 by 1994. Any move by the Maasai to reduce their livestock herds in favour of increased cultivation would inevitably lead to further confrontation between

*One of Ngorongoro's more unusual inhabitants – the porcupine.*

the wildlife and the farmers. In some cases families are in dire economic and nutritional circumstances because of livestock losses.

Traditionally the Maasai and their cattle are indivisible. Their livestock have always comingled with wildlife without any problems other than the occasional lion or leopard confrontation. The Maasai moran live mostly on milk, blood, and meat supplied by their cattle, supplemented by maize, potatoes, and beans, which form the main diet of the women and children. The vegetable requirements for such a comparatively small population are modest and can easily be catered for, and in the past were provided by trade with non-Maasai agricultural tribes, many of whom were invited to cultivate in what is now the NCA.

A top priority for the NCA is to assist the Maasai to build up their cattle population. This would be beneficial to everybody, and would help them retain their pastoral interest rather than becoming agriculturists like their cousins in the Arusha area, the Waarusha, thus greatly diminishing the present trend towards increased and often unlawful clearing for agriculture resulting in inevitable conflict with wildlife.

Improved veterinary services, particularly increased dipping against tick-borne diseases, are therefore a top priority. Although veterinary services have improved over recent years, they are inadequate to meet the demand, and residents are particularly concerned about the scarcity and expense of veterinary drugs.

Food security issues include the question of how to enhance the pastoral tradition amongst residents, and how to manage cultivation while protecting the conservation values for which the NCA was originally established.

The 1975 act which established the NCAA included a specific ban on cultivation within the area. Non-indigenous residents were, and still are, continuing illegal cultivation in spite of periodic crackdowns, in violation of both the 1975 act and the prime minister's directive to protect the area. Conservationists fear that uncontrolled cultivation will continue to encourage illegal immigration into the NCA and undermine the ecological integrity of the area.

Unlike the compatible coexistence of livestock and wild animals, the cultivation of food crops in game areas invariably leads to shamba (farm) raiding by game, particularly buffalo and elephant. A small shamba can easily be devastated in a few hours, as often happened when I was farming in Karatu. This leads to conflict between the animals and the cultivators, resulting in necessary control measures by wildlife or national park game scouts. Often, unavoidably, it is necessary to kill when all other methods, such as shooting over the top of their heads or using thunderflash fireworks, fail to drive off the animals concerned.

The problems tackled by the NCA and the Serengeti National Park are similar to those existing throughout the world where wildlife projects exist, particularly in Africa.

*A pair of lions devour a carcass while other scavengers wait their turn.*

*A guided walking safari allows more intimate contact with the environment than the confines of a vehicle.*

*The bloated stomachs of these lions show that they are well fed and ready for a siesta.*

*In a dramatic moment, a hyena snatches a wildebeest foal from under the very nose of its mother.*

*A silver-backed jackal explores a feather.*

*Jackal cubs huddle together for protection.*

National parks, game reserves, and other game-protected areas have to compete with the continual pressure of an ever-increasing human population. The basic needs of the indigenous people for food, land, and water understandably have priority over wildlife.

Tribesmen living along the boundaries of game-protected areas are often undernourished. Formerly, before the white man arrived in Africa, introducing firearms, the people there used bows and arrows, spears, and game traps to hunt animals for their food. There were always plenty of animals around to fill the larder and replace those hunted and killed, and the balance worked perfectly for both man and animal. With the arrival of the white man a century or so ago, and the carve-up of the African continent by the European powers into 'spheres of influence', everything quickly changed. Intertribal warfare and many of the worst diseases that had ensured the survival of only the fittest were to a large extent eliminated. Muzzle-loaders were superseded by rifles and then machine guns as firearms became increasingly sophisticated. New roads and modern vehicles have opened up game areas to poachers armed with modern weapons who have, in many places, virtually wiped out some species.

Admittedly, the Maasai themselves in the NCA cannot be accused of this wholesale poaching which exists elsewhere, but they do utilize the game corridor to the west of the crater. This corridor is used by many species during the migration, particularly wildebeest, zebra, Thomson's gazelle, and eland. There has been increasing pastoral settlement in the area which, together with the illegal cultivation, may well obstruct and affect the migration flow.

Another more recent project that encourages local people to participate in game conservation is the Serengeti Regional Conservation Strategy (SRCS), which concerns the agricultural peoples west of the Serengeti National Park.

There are up to 30,000 illegal hunters operating there, providing meat to the million people living within 45 kilometres (28 miles) of the western boundary of the park. Although difficult to establish the take-off figures, it has been established that these poachers account for about 200,000 animals a year, inside and outside the park. Obviously this harvest is unsustainable, and some areas within the park are already devoid of game.

The SRCS is attempting to replace the illegal hunting in the park with a legalized cull outside the park. Another proposal is that an animal husbandry scheme should be introduced, supplying meat from domestic animals at a lower cost than illegal, poached game meat.

The success, or otherwise, of these control measures will determine the future of the present ongoing annual migration of some two million animals. In turn, if this migration, which has survived thousands, if not millions of years, does not survive, the future of the animals in the Ngorongoro Crater is also in jeopardy.

*A large family of young ostrich.*

Picture by: Tom Lithgow (Jnr)

*This tusker, a recent arrival in the crater, is the largest seen there fore many years. It is estimated that each tusk weighs about 40 Kilograms (90 pounds).*

# BIBLIOGRAPHY

Barns, T.A. *Across the Great Craterland to the Congo*. Ernest Benn Ltd, 1923.

Baumann, Oscar. *Durch Masailand zur Nilquelle*. Berlin, 1894. (Trans. Organ, H., and Fosbrooke, H.A., East African Literature Bureau, 1963.)

Fourie, Gert. Unpublished diary.

Government of Tanganyika. 'The Serengeti National Park.' Government Printer, Dar es Salaam, 1956.

Government of Tanganyika. 'The Serengeti Committee of Inquiry.' Government Printer, Dar es Salaam, 1957.

Government of Tanganyika. 'Proposals for Reconstituting the Serengeti National Park.' Government Printer, Dar es Salaam, 1958.

Holmes, F. Radcliffe. *Interviewing Wild Animals*. Stanley Martin & Co., London, 1929.

Leakey, L.S.B. *Stone Ages of Kenya*. Oxford University Press, 1934.

Leakey, M. 'Memorandum on Neolithic Grave Excavations in the Ngorongoro.' Unpublished, 1941.

Oetker, Ursula, and Kaselowsky, Richard. 'Ngorongoro.' Privately published.

Reck, Hans. *Oldoway, die Schlucht des Urmenschen*. F.V. Brockhaus, Leipzig, 1952.

Sinclair, A.R.E., and Arcese, Peter, eds. *Serengeti II: Dynamics, Management, and Conservation of an Ecosystem*. University of Chicago Press, Chicago and London, 1995.

Thomson, Joseph. *Through Maasailand*. Sampson Low, Marston, Searle & Rivington, London, 1885.

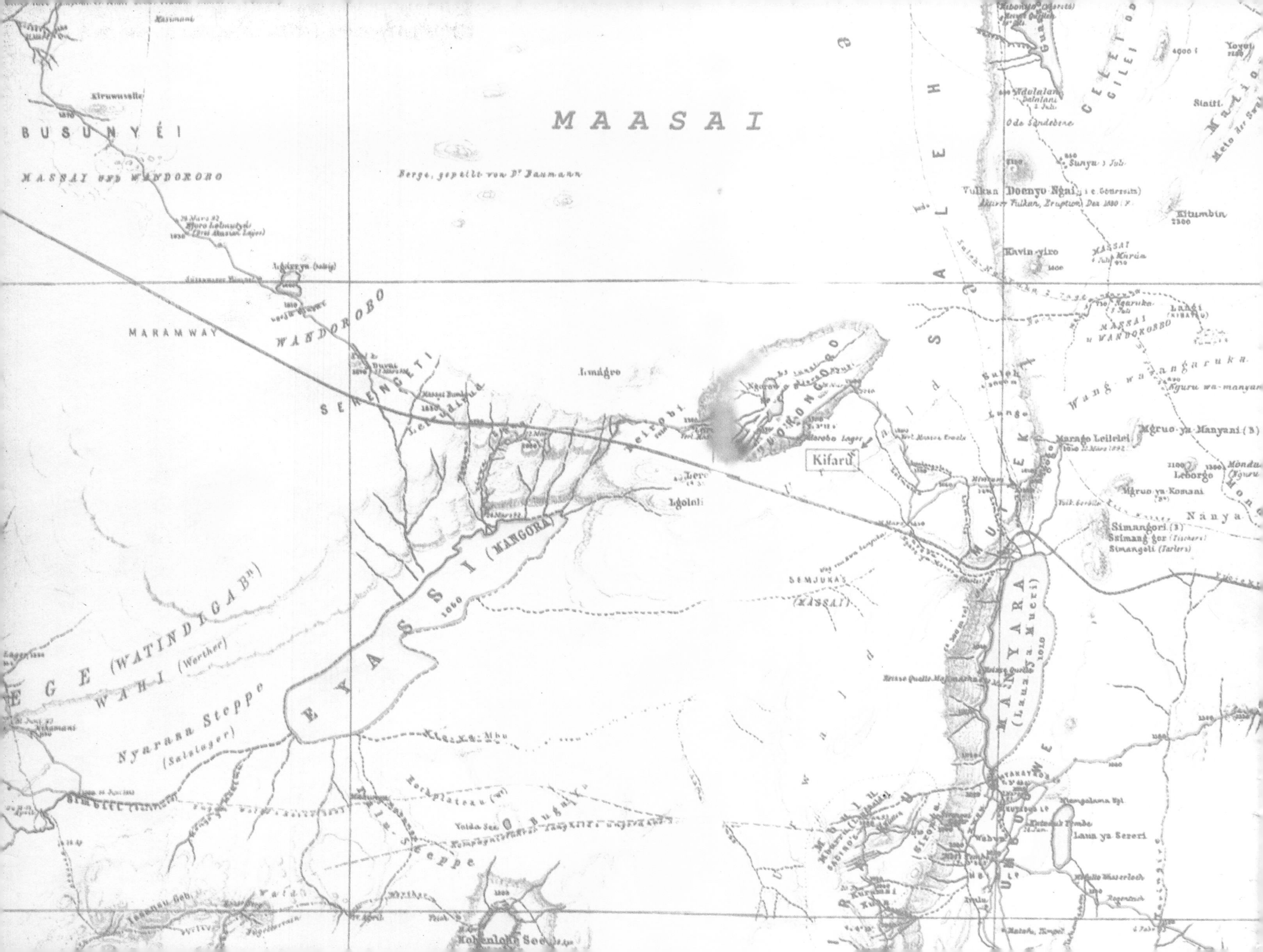

MAASAI
BUSUNYÉI
MASSAI UND WANDOROBO
Berge, gepeilt von Dr Baumann
MARAMWAY
WANDOROBO
SERENGETI
Lmagro
Kifaru
Lgolol
Vulkan Doenyo Ngai
Kitumbin
Kavin-yiro
Sunyu
Ndulalan
Langi
MASSAI u WANDOROBBO
Wang wa Angaruka
Mgruo ya Manyani
Marago Leilelei
Leborgo
Mgruo ya Komani
Nanya
Simangori
Simangeli
SEMJUKAS (MASSAI)
EYASSI (MANGORA)
1060
EGE (WATINDIGA)
WAHI (Werther)
Nyarasa Steppe
(Salzlager)
MANYARA (Laua ya Mueri)
1010
Laua ya Sereri
Kohenlohe See

# MAURITIUS STYLE

Endpapers: *Coco Beach Hotel. The vast parasol roof of the Coco Beach Hotel is reminiscent of the marquees built for the balls given by the governors in the colonial period. The most memorable is the ball held in 1800 in the gardens of government house, where the invitations were posted using the famous 'Blue Penny' stamp.*

Page 4: *Villa Caroline. This simple family guesthouse on the west coast has been developed into a small hotel which has used elements of traditional architecture.*

Pages 6-7: *At the mouth of the Tamarin River a local 'pirogue' glides through the calm waters in the late afternoon sun.*

Pages 8-9: *The bright red flowers of the flame trees stand out against the landscape of calm blue-grey and discreet green.*

Translated from the French by Isabelle Desvaux de Marigny and Henriette Valentin Lagesse

First published in Mauritius in 1991 by
Les Nouvelles Editions du Pacifique
Reprinted 1992, 1994

This new revised edition published in 2002 by Archipelago Press,
an imprint of Editions Didier Millet,
121 Telok Ayer Street, #03-01, Singapore 068590
www.edmbooks.com

Printed in Singapore

ISBN: 981-4068-49-7

# MAURITIUS STYLE
## Life on the Verandah

Preface
*Geneviève Dormann*

Photographs
*Christian Vaisse*

Introduction
*Christian Saglio*

Text and captions
*Isabelle Desvaux de Marigny* and *Henriette Valentin Lagesse*

with the collaboration of
*Jean-François Kœnig*

ARCHIPELAGO PRESS

# CONTENTS

8

Above: *The mountains of Mauritius have always impressed travellers, inspiring descriptions such as "vast pocket Matterhorns" or "fantastic peaks...as if nature had been in a merry mood at the time of their creation".*

Left: *Sugar harvesting has always been hard manual labour; the introduction of machines is a comparatively recent event.*

Above: *One can almost hear the crackle of burning cane, a practice that facilitates harvesting.*

Right: *The primitive ox-drawn cart is a rare sight in the days of the modernised sugar industry.*

Above: *Jules Leclerc once said that if Mauritius is the paradise of the southern hemisphere, the Pamplemousses gardens are the paradise of Mauritius...*
Left: *These giant water lilies are the gardens' major attraction. They open in the afternoon and close the following morning. On the first day they are white, and on the second they are pink.*

Labourdonnais purchased the Mon Plaisir
Estate in 1735 and created a kitchen
garden that would provide for his staff, the
growing population of Port-Louis and for
the crews of passing ships.
The Pamplemousses Gardens were
originally conceived as a nursery where
plants of botanical or economic interest
imported from Europe or the East could be
acclimatised. In 1768 Mon Plaisir was sold
to M. Poivre. It was he, in fact, who was the
true creator of the Pamplemousses
Gardens; under his ownership they became
a centre of exchange for plants from all
around the world.
Right: The grand entrance gates, donated
by Mr François Liénard de Lamivoye, won
an award at the Word Exposition of
London in 1851.

14

# ON THE VERANDAH

Look carefully at the pictures in this superb album. They are precious because they pay tribute to the houses of Mauritius which we, perhaps, may be the last to know if the government of this country does not take the precautions necessary to preserve its heritage. Most of these houses are now more than a hundred years old; they tell of the efforts of a people to live harmoniously, struggling against the dangers of the sea, against the winds and the rain, and against time.

Their design, colours and fine decoration are inspired by the Orient, Africa and the Western world, creating a poetry that is far more moving than the photographs of Mauritius currently used by the advertising industry to promote package holidays. Within the pages of this book you will not find pictures of palm-fringed beaches or fluorescent swimming pools incarcerated in those concrete, air-conditioned hotels that are inevitably the same, from the Caribbean to the Bahamas, from the African coast to the holiday paradises of the Far East.

The human being features little amongst these pages, and yet they trace the story of two centuries of ingenuity and imagination, combining the basics for human survival with everyday comfort and poetry.

The book is also a cry for help, the second to my knowledge, appearing twelve years after Jean Louis Pagès' book, *Maisons Traditionelles de l'Île Maurice* (Editions de l'Océan Indien). His illustrations aimed to champion the cause of the beautiful Mauritian houses — both patrician and popular — whose enormous charm

attracts the admiration of travellers from around the world. Indeed, with the vast tourism market now available to holiday-makers, the day of the single-minded sun-worshipper is passing. More and more, tourists want to discover the character and the soul, that is the history, of the country they visit. The remains of their heritage.

They prefer to stay in typical houses rather than hotels that are of an identical mould from one end of the planet to the other. Architects in Mauritius have just begun to realise this and are now beginning to build hotels which feature Creole-style bungalows.

Virtually every year a cyclone passes through the island, destroying vegetation and houses, only for the houses to be replaced by terrible concrete. Blocks dumped on the same spot, under a flat slab in guise of a roof, their walls punctuated by coffin-like windows, with thick grills to deter supposed burglars. Thus the concrete epidemic which raged in the sixties has ravaged parts of Mauritius, razing many beautiful houses that were still habitable, to replace them by sad constructions considered to be practical and rational by urban planners with no sense of aesthetics. At Port-Louis, the remains of beautiful eighteenth-century French architecture are being demolished to make way for buildings that are more profitable given the price of land in the middle of the town. At this very moment a group of Mauritian architects are begging the government to spare two ancient monuments on the Place des Armes; one of them, now the home of the national mint, was the bakery that sold biscuits and bread to the trading fleets on their way to the West Indies at the time of Labourdonnais.

This haste to destroy also derives — whether consciously or not — from a will to suppress all traces of European presence in Mauritius. The beautiful "colonial style" houses are actually the last vestiges of Creole architecture, based on two centuries of experience of living in the tropics. These houses, the beautiful houses

pictured in this book, are at the risk of becoming, in our lifetime, mere memories.

Arguments to replace them with concrete are not convincing. It is obvious that wood is more fragile and requires more upkeep. Yet these well-loved old houses have nonetheless resisted, the majority of them for more than a century, the ravages of cyclones. Their sloping roofs keep out the heaviest rain and create a protective cushion of air above the living quarters, whereas the concrete roofs-cum-terraces are not totally watertight and are subject to an unfavourable thermal inertia: they retain the heat of the day and emit it during the night; patches of damp appear. The centre of Curepipe is thus disgraced by hideous blocks whose sides are streaked with long green water stains.

Over two centuries, the Mauritians have learned to build their houses to cope with the winds and the rain, the heat and the light. The first cases of Port-Louis were simple wooden boxes, roughly hewn and without foundations; they were often moved, in pieces or as a whole on rollers. Oiled paper served as glass for the windows. Shelter was not guaranteed: water would pour in when the rain was heavy. Under Mahé de Bourdonnais stone began to feature and some homes took on, in his memory, a Breton aspect. The beautiful Robillard family home at Mahébourg, now a museum, could easily have been built at Saint Malo or Saint-Servant.

Only later, with the arrival of the English, did comfort become a consideration. But wood remained the favoured material of the boatbuilders who were also responsible for building the first houses during the years of French rule on Mauritius.

There is a seaside "campement" on the west coast with walls of ravenala, a palm also known as "arbre du voyageur". These walls, made of layers of leaves, seem to be light and fragile. Yet the house stands up to cyclones for the simple

reason that the the winds, instead of hitting it, go through it without harm. It is an effective symbol. Perhaps the same goes for life, and it is better to let yourself be buffeted by bad squalls than to oppose them with a rigid and inflexible mind. The first inhabitants of the island left traces of their vocabulary both in its architecture and its language. So we have the word "varangue" to describe the most important and the most appealing place in the Mauritian house. This word, that slips so easily off the tongue...is it a corruption of "veranda"? I prefer to associate it with the French word "varangue", denoting the piece of wood that protects the hull of a ship.

The verandah, place of passage and repose, surrounding or extending the house, is both sitting room and garden, an intermediary space between interior and exterior. It is a filter between the intimacy of the family sanctuary and the unknown of the outside world. It is on the verandah that people receive a visitor and get to know him before allowing him to perpetrate to the heart of the home. It is a place of delicacy, of welcome but also of precaution. An invisible portcullis separates the verandah from the rest of the house.

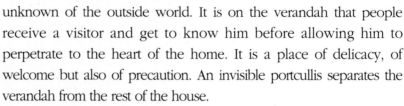

For the people who live there, it is also an observation post. A true sailor is always looking out of the window of his house, either to check his boat at its mooring, or to watch out for invasion by the enemy. Even if he has no boat to tend, even if the enemy is not likely to appear over the horizon, the Mauritian islander always has a wandering eye, and the verandah is his domain. Hence the relatively large number of people who claim to have seen the celebrated green light, just before sunset. The green light is a product of the verandah. It is a place for the curious, where noises outside and movements of the neighbours can be heard. Nothing escapes the verandah where, in the shade of ferns and allamandas,

through the chinks of lowered blinds, the observer can see everything without being seen. Shaded against the sun, the heat of midday becomes bearable, while the little geckos, the good fairies of the verandah, fasten the suction pads of their feet to the walls and, with beating heart, swallow flies and mosquitoes with a well-aimed flick of the tongue. It is a place for relaxation where, even on the most sultry days, a light breeze skips across polished floors, an invisible fan to soothe burning foreheads.

The verandah is a place for dreams and gossip. The confidences of the verandah, always whispered, are tinted with the pastel shades of dawn, the gold of sunsets.

> *Aux pays du sucre et des mangues*
> *Les pales dames créoles*
> *S'eventent sous les farangues*
> *Au pays du sucre et des mangues*
> *Et zézaient de lentes paroles.*
> *(In the land of sugar and mangoes*
> *The pale Creole ladies*
> *Fan themselves under the verandahs*
> *In the land of sugar and mangoes*
> *And slowly lisp their words.)*
> Paul Jean Toulet, *Vers Inédits* (Bouquins Robert Laffont)

To live on the verandah is to choose to preserve, amidst our violent and nervous world, an interlude of grace and serenity. It is everything that we love.

Geneviève Dormann

# THE FATE OF THE DODO?

Cap Malheureux, Crève-Coeur, Solitude, Baie du Tombeau, Pétrin, Grande Retraite, Fond du Sac…Land in Mauritius and plunge into its atmosphere of nostalgia, letting the names of towns and houses run through your mind and evoke their images according to the mood of the moment: Espérance, L'Aventure, Cachette, Providence, Trou aux Biches, Sans Souci, Poudre d'Or, Trou d'Eau Douce, Mon Repos, Bois d'Amourettes, Flic en Flac, Trou Fanfaron, Coin de Mire, Bel Ombre, Tour de l'Harmonie, Beaux Songes, Mon Désert-Mon Trésor…

The map of Mauritius reads like a poem, at times joyful, at times melancholy. I remember, as a child, that President Senghor once gave me a copy and I hung it on my bedroom wall where it remained long after. It was a constant reminder of how the president used it to illustrate his theories, declaring solemnly, "the Future and the Centre of the Universe are here!" He was no doubt alluding to the famous cultural and biological mixture produced by the charming melting pot that is Mauritius. This promised land has received the seeds of an incongruous multitude of races, religions and lifestyles from all the corners of the

*Left: The statue of Mahé de Labourdonnais presides over the Place du Quai, Port-Louis.*
*Above: The old central market in Curepipe was built in 1917 by M Maurice Loumeau. It was destroyed in 1976.*

earth. There might even be scope here for the in-vitro fertilisation of a "Universal Civilisation". Having immersed myself in this extraordinary maelstrom for a period of three years, I tend to agree with the president-cum-poet — who is also a member of the Académie Française.

But that is another story. My aim here is not to discuss the future of the Mauritian cultural kaleidoscope but to examine one of its most distinctive ingredients: the houses.

## PLANET OF THE LITTLE PRINCE

On this "planet of the Little Prince, where all your dreams may come true"*, the houses are a

part of the mirage. Each is unique and yet part of a harmonious whole. From the impressive residences of Curepipe to the small shops of Port-Louis, they combine a variety of influences, bearing witness to the panache and fantasy of a complex way of life that combines eighteenth century Versailles, British cosiness, African rhythm and Oriental mystery. Houses have been conceived to adapt to the ever-changing climate of an island where technicoloured rainbows divide the sky and where, at any time of day, and at any place or altitude, the traveller can pass in less than half an hour from a real London fog to the blue sea and blazing sun of the tourist brochures.

The *varangue* or verandah is the only defence against these charming inconsistencies. An intrinsic, and almost metaphysical, part of the Mauritian soul, the verandah plays the many roles of entrance, hall, terrace, tearoom, deck and conservatory. The verandah has a whole way of life of its own: the play of light and shade determined by the raising and lowering of raffia blinds which are painted the same colour as the shingled roof. The very word "varangue" becomes as essential to the foreign traveller as it is to the old native. A house in the garden and a garden in the house... this is what

*Antoine de St-Exupéry, *Le Petit Prince*, Hachette, 1945.

*The verandah at Le Réduit is festooned with tropical greenery.*

*Mr Henri Harel's house in Curepipe, next to the Town Hall. It was demolished in the fifties (photo 1927).*

verandah living is all about. It is a century-old way of life that continues still: I will always cherish dearly the memory of those dear old ladies who welcomed me on the *varangue* of their large wooden homes.

Mauritian houses are evocative of ships... Built by naval carpenters, they retained the spirit, appearance and framework of a ship and they seem ready to set sail at any moment. Baudelaire, whose famous poem *A une dame créole* was inspired by Mauritius, maintained that "décrire c'est dégrader et se dégrader"*. I will therefore avoid writing a descriptive inventory which takes account of the least important door handle. The photographs that follow are sufficiently eloquent. It can only be hoped that the superb images contained in this book will not become the sole remaining testimony to an architecture submerged by a tide of concrete.

## THE PROMISED LAND

Mauritius has its origins in every corner of the globe. On arrival, the traveller's first impression is one of recognition rather than discovery, a feeling which probably stems from the global ancestry of the island. After solving the riddles of the map (strangely reminiscent of childhood treasure hunts), I immediately recognised the familiar faces of the mountains transformed into human beings by Malcolm de Chazal, the surrealist author (according to whom, "On Mauritius, we cultivate sugar cane and preconceptions"); the gentle and chaste waterfalls of *Paul et Virginie;* the pirates and buccaneers of *Treasure Island;* the deserted coves haunted by Robinson Crusoe; the blue lagoons of picture postcards; and the houses straight out of *Gone with the Wind....* all those places I had

*"To describe is to degrade and to degrade oneself."

The Hôtel de Ville of Curepipe with, in the foreground, the well-loved statue of Paul and Virginie.

long cherished in my imagination before I finally came across them in reality.

Behind the stereotypes — landscapes created for the setting for a popular musical or to be reproduced on holiday postcards — are traces of days gone by. One can still feel the strange and powerful fascination of forgotten worlds, man being, after all, but a brief incident in the history of this very old piece of land. Millions of years had elapsed before the arrival, only a few centuries ago, of the first navigators, the Arabs, the Portuguese and the Dutch. The explorers were followed by corsairs and gentlemen farmers from Brittany, the younger sons of titled families who came in the hope of finding fame and fortune in the tropics. Then it was the turn of the bands of suffering slaves uprooted from Africa or Madagascar. Only in 1810 (after the British landing at Cap Malheureux) did British soldiers and civil servants — dilettantes and fair-play denizens — begin to settle. Thereafter came successive waves of immigrants, mostly tradesmen and agricultural workers from China and the Indian sub-continent.

During the first three hundred years of settlement in this promised land, man had managed to preserve a balance with nature. The absence of humanity for so long can still be felt strongly in many parts of the island. But recently it would seem that the human machine has lost control and that the traditional Mauritian houses are to be its first victims.

*Above left: Tea at Britannia Savanne. From left: T W Innes, J G Gibson, A Mac Millan, Mrs Innes.*
*Above right: The sitting room at Chateaufort (photo 1932).*

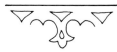

## Ephemeral, Alas...

I have always admired the grace of things ephemeral — except in the case of houses. When he is wandering in foreign parts, the traveller depends on his ports of call. Fortunately for him, houses must remain where they are. In his nomadic existence of comings and goings, voyages, encounters, departures, rediscoveries and more or less final goodbyes, houses are the only constant landmarks and retreats.

The wooden houses of Mauritius are, by nature, ephemeral. Here, more than elsewhere, "les maisons sont fugitives, hélas, comme les années..."* (Baudelaire). Precariously poised between past and present, they need to be loved to survive the ravages of cyclones, termites and, above all, property developers.

## Atmosphere, Atmosphere

"Objets inanimés, auriez-vous donc une âme?..."**(Baudelaire) These old wooden houses throb and breathe and warp and shrink; in short, they live. Modern houses are rarely

capable of inspiring dreams.

Why this passion for the Mauritian "painted ladies" (a term of endearment often applied to San Francisco's wooden houses), this dogged determination not to compromise when they are threatened? Why this irresistible urge to cross their threshold, to discover their secrets, to invade and conquer them? Why this need to understand them and to be adopted by them? Perhaps because there emanates from them a disquieting atmosphere, redolent of both sensuality and spirituality, a charm that captures the imagination and the soul.

Their reputation of being haunted comes from their touching combination of strength and vulnerability. They appear suddenly round the corner of a drive, their blue-shingled roofs

*"Houses, alas, are as fleeting as time itself... "
**"Lifeless objects, might there yet be a soul in you?"
(Baudelaire)

*Above centre: Destruction at Montalieu, Curepipe, following cyclone Carol (photo 1960).*
*Above right: View of a house at the foot of Moka hill (engraving by Milbert).*

set against a backdrop of sky and mountains, like wafting, insubstantial ghosts but always rooted in the most perfect location. These houses are the stuff of which our dreams are made: we recognise them at once. But we must learn to keep peace with them, to respect them and to listen to them before they exclude us from their secrets forever.

It is difficult to determine exactly why one is moved by certain places and certain people. Perhaps it is due to those minute peculiarities which reflect their deeper nature, or because of some mysterious affinity which creates the magic of a meeting. One has only to isolate the components of charm in order to become immune to it. Yet, although I have studied and

*Above right: The entrance hall at Mongoust (reconstruction by Jean Lejuge de Segrais).*

examined them for a long time, the houses of Mauritius continue to seduce me. I almost share the common belief that they are haunted. Within these houses I have often sensed more mystery and esoteric animism than in the depths of the sacred forests of Africa.

The old wooden houses are never completely silent. Each one has its own orchestration of sounds. They may reassure you or disturb you but they always keep you company. Creaks, whispers, hushes, gasps, squeaks, footsteps...a multitude of signs and signals enliven the solemn silence of these houses "where foot-steps have a meaning..." (Baudelaire).

## BRIEF ENCOUNTERS

I feel that I have met some of these houses in the same way that one meets people; they have just as much to tell. Houses permeated my life in Mauritius and dwelt in me just as I dwelt in them.

It is hard to describe these encounters: memories flood through my mind pell-mell after umpteen moves from house to house. I changed house ten times in three years and, whether big or small, I loved each house in a different way.

Château la Misère at Cap Malheureux; the

*Above left: The former convent of the Sisters of Lorette in Port-Louis nestles at the foot of the citadel.*
*Above right: Mongoust in the days of its glory (photo 1883).*

Résidence Bagatelle at Mon Désert-Mon Trésor; Villa Mon Désir at Flic en Flac; Maison Mon Goût at Grande Retraite; the islands: Pourquoi Pas?; Mouchoir Rouge; Deux Cocos. I devised a game with these addresses and could not resist writing

them in turn (except for the islands and Flic en Flac) on my Parisian cheques. I enjoyed the consternation of petrol attendants on French motorways who would ask without fail: "Are you sure this can be cashed in France?"

## LA MALMAISON

In 1903, La Malmaison was moved from Moka to Curepipe to be used as the Town Hall. This was in the days when houses were often displaced with the purchase of a new property or as the result of a marriage or an epidemic.

La Malmaison was my first encounter with a Mauritian house and, in many ways, it remains the most spectacular. I came across it on a typically gloomy and wet Curepipe afternoon, the day after my arrival in Mauritius, when it appeared like a ghost out of the drizzly mist so suggestive of Brittany...an abandoned wreck, its

limbs still quivering...as if in the final throes of death.

Reality only affects us when it begins to embody our fantasies, when our imagination is captured by certainty. "Do these fairy-tale houses really exist?...", I asked myself. Facing this queen of Mauritian houses, I was reminded of all the castles of my child-hood dreams, of *Gone with the Wind* and *Sleeping Beauty* ."Home, home...", like ET, I was back home at last. I responded to the call of the house.

On my first day I had fallen for this queen, tattered but still resplendent with dignity and elegance. Surrounded by building sites, a bus stop, a nightmarish Hotel Europa, a casino, a stupefying covered market (originally destined to be an aquarium in Belgium, if Curepipian gossip is to be believed), La Malmaison has managed to preserve her forsaken majesty.

The fervent advocates of concrete were apparently disappointed that the last cyclones did not succeed in "doing away once and for all with the problematic Town Hall." They had plans for a wonderful five-storey building to take its place. But La Malmaison has survived worse threats and is now awaiting renovation.

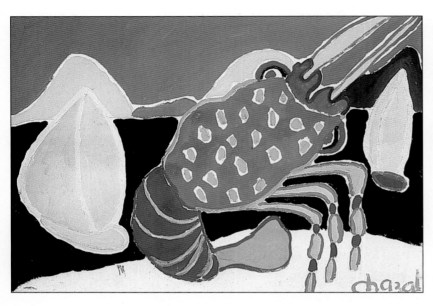

## La Rocherie

The Maison Carné, donated to the church by the Comtesse de Carné, was my second encounter. I entered it as one does a sanctuary, just before the heirs sold off to the highest bidder the furniture and every trace of the old Comtesse (who died at the age of 103!). It was an almost sacrilegious stripping down during which all the contents of the house, including photograph albums, mirrored wardrobes, curtain rails and large enamelled baths with griffins' feet, were dispersed, along with all the memories and the very atmosphere of the place. Immediately before the kill, everything was in its place, just as in the good old days, and I could not resist the temptation of pushing the ivory button of the mahogany bellpull that was hanging over the bed. The bell still rang in the pantry, like a voice from the past.

## Eureka

"It is to this house, the most important place for my family, that I must now return... A mythical house to me as I only ever heard of it in terms of a lost house... White, light, standing against a range of mountains whose names seemed magical to me: Le Pouce, les Deux Mamelles, le Pieter Both... No other house will ever be so

important, no other will ever possess such a soul...vast and silent amidst the secret solitude of its earthly paradise, retaining in its heart the remembrance of its birth, like a place to which one never returns?" (J.M.G. Le Clézio, *Voyages à Rodrigues*, Journal Gallimard, 1985)

Euréka has been saved from demolition. "The great wooden house with its hundred French windows" has been turned into a museum. You can have lunch there on the large verandah and listen to your host recount endless anecdotes about the Le Clézio family.

The lengthy and extravagant saga is rather like "Dallas in Moka". Euréka's history is composed of a Balzacian world with eccentric, all-powerful great-aunts, disputes over acres of sugar cane, divisions of factories, squandered rupees, solicitors and legacies.

## POURQUOI PAS?

An island within the island of Mauritius, Pourquoi Pas? is an island-house that floats capriciously (why not?...) in the middle of the Roches Noires lagoon. I had often sailed around it before finally landing and spending some time there.

It is a sunny weekend refuge from the mists of the upper plateau. I loved its makeshift and casual appearance, defying the sedate concrete of the seaside *campements*. (The term "campement" originally referred to a weekend house made of ravenala and straw. Whole families — and most of their belongings — used to move from the upper plateau to "go camping" in the summer months. Nowadays, the word is applied to the ever-multiplying concrete villas that house the tourists.) I also loved its frayed filaos, its tall verandah patched up after each cyclone and its half-hidden approach via a wobbly old pontoon stretched over the turquoise lagoon. On Pourquoi Pas?, one has only to turn one's head to watch the setting of the sun and the rising of the moon on the same evening: a rare privilege in Mauritius.

Not far from here is the St Geran channel, the site of the famous shipwreck that was immortalised in Bernadin de St Pierre's novel *Paul et Virginie*. Virginie, draped in her virginity, dies at the prow of the sinking ship amid the foaming waves, a tragic victim of her modesty. This is more than the melodramatic, flowery and exotic novelette that some censors would have us believe. To be carried away into an almost

*Above centre: The statue of Paul and Virginie at Curepipe.*
*Above left: Maison Blanche.*

biblical paradise by its chaste eroticism, the reader should turn its pages on this very stretch of water, between the islands of Pourquoi Pas? and Ambre.

## VILLA CAYEUX

"Diplomat looking for large wooden house..." This small advertisement went against the trend of all the others which abound in the Mauritian daily newspapers: "Prestigious concrete villa to let"..."To sell:  excellent wood from demolished property". My advertisement was deliberately

provocative in the context of an era when many beautiful houses were condemned or moribund, awaiting the fate of those which had already disappeared. It led to some memorable encounters with houses and their owners, who have since become my friends.

As soon as I set foot upon its creaking floorboards, I fell in love with the Villa Cayeux and began to try to comprehend it. Our idyll lasted for a year. The house was elegant and melancholy, with its ornate wrought-iron balustrade, its colonnaded verandah and its sky-blue roof (of that nondescript and sublime blue that is particular only to Curepipe when, for once, it does not rain). The same pastel shades prevailed in the garden: the mauves, blues, pinks and whites of hydrangeas, begonias, camelias, orchids, azaleas and lily of the valley. Inside, the pastel world continued. This house was my refuge: I felt completely at home amidst its faded wallpapers, its crystal chandeliers, its four-poster beds, its mirrored wardrobes, its ever-extendable dining table, its easy chairs, sideboards, sofas, pedestal tables, consoles, upholstered armchairs and writing desks... There was a whole series of large dimly-lit rooms with creaking floorboards and communicating doors whose handles were made of brass or crystal. One of these doors led to an incongruous early-thirties bathroom with shiny green ceramic tiles which looked almost

*Above: Villa Cayeux has been dismantled to be rebuilt on the island of Deux Cocos.*

good enough to eat!

In this house prowled a rather distant and austere presence, known by visiting friends as "the ghost". We built up an excellent working relationship that was both considerate and demanding. He knew how

to test us and manifested himself through a profusion of sounds and an avalanche of coded messages. I would fall asleep to the muffled sound of rain streaming down the roof and would be awakened by silence. I would lie listening to the house...was someone walking in the attic, or breathing behind the door, or was the ghost simply disappearing into the bedroom wardrobe? A haunted house generally mirrors one's own dreams...

After the death of its owner, the Villa Cayeux was to be demolished and replaced by soulless — and ghostless — blocks of flats. It was saved by an unbelievable stroke of luck and has been dismantled with great care, plank by plank, to be rebuilt on the island of Deux Cocos, where it will have a new lease on life. (This used to be a fairly regular occurrence in Mauritius. Houses would be moved as new properties were acquired, when people were married or when epidemics threatened. Nowadays, houses are rarely displaced, the last case being the Curepipe Town Hall — in 1903.) As for the Villa Cayeux, I wish it as happy a transplantation as as that of the Scottish ghost in René Clair's film *Ghost for Sale*. Deported to California, it wandered as a lost soul until (the typically happy Hollywood ending) its reincarnation and marriage to a rich heiress.

## PELL-MELL

It is impossible to describe all my encounters; each Mauritian house has its own personality and atmosphere, its stories and anecdotes. Although they are not invulnerable, they are inexhaustible story-tellers.

I will conclude pell-mell with a medley of impressions: Château Guimbeau at the entrance to Curepipe, like a reward after the slow crawl from Plaisance* airport, sandwiched between smoky buses and rows of concrete structures promoting Pepsi and Coca Cola; the small

*"Plaisance" was an auspicious name for an airport, but, like the Pamplemousses Gardens, it has been renamed Sir Seewoosagur Ramgoolam Airport, in memory of the Father of Independence.

fisherman's house on the island of Mouchoir Rouge adrift on Mahébourg, the loveliest lagoon of Mauritius; the rectory of the Immaculate Conception in Port-Louis where Père Souchon invited me to discover the marvellous attic and where I first fell in love with the indefinable grey-green Wedgwood blue which has since become my favourite colour; Sorèze House whose colonnades are hidden behind a romantic copse; the Hôtel International, last refuge of Malcolm de Chazal, with its antique ceiling fans and its map of France dating from the fifties; the Point de Vénus, beaten by the trade winds, atop a hill on the small island of Rodriguès (600 kilometres east of Mauritius), basking in the old world atmosphere of a kind of Irish Africa where polkas, waltzes and quadrilles are still

the order of the day at village fairs; la Sablonnière, now the "Le Gourmet" restaurant (arrive there in the evening, preferably under a tropical downpour so that the maître d'hôtel will come out with an umbrella to meet you at the foot of the steps, before you dine looking out over an Eiffel Tower (built in 1889) that rises — like a hallucination — from between two palm trees; the island of Deux Cocos and its turn-of-the-century folly, a neo-Moorish patio of pink, rough-cut colonnades and arcades set on the white sands of Blue Bay; La Tour Blanche, looming over the waterfalls of the valley of Beau-Bassin whence, so the legend goes, Darwin set off astride an elephant (imported from India) on his search to prove his theory of evolution; Villa Wiehe in Floréal, the most

*Above: The verandah at Chateaufort exudes elegance and dignity.*
*Above right: Constructed in 1870, the Royal Alfred Observatory was abandoned in 1959 and demolished soon after.*

reserved and charming of all the Mauritian homes I discovered, like a face whose features are not immediately striking, but whose impression grows on you and never leaves you... So many houses, so many encounters, so many anecdotes...

The following houses are but a more few that cannot be omitted from my lengthy honours list: Château Trompette with its long drive and turrets, Béthanie with its "escarpolette", *varangue* and fountain, and, last but not least, the large Moolan residence on the Champ de

*Above: "Some Mauritian houses" from A Mac Millan's* Mauritius Illustrated *(London, 1914).*

Mars, Bel Air, Surprise, Saint Antoine, Esperanza, Belle Vue, Le Mesnil, Mauricia, the Harel houses in Curepipe, Riche en Eau, Le Coconut, La Villebague, Champrosay, Labourdonnais, Mon Rêve, Beau Séjour, the Monte Carlo guest house, Poncini, Verdun, La Tour Koenig, Bel Ombre, L'Arbre Rouge, the Geber House, the naval museum at Mahébourg and all those houses that still hold out against the concrete invasion that is threatening Vacoas, Curepipe, Quatre Bornes, Phoenix or Rose Hill. I must also commend the Plaza Theatre (1934) and the theatre at Port-Louis where strange echoes are created by the wooden auditoriums.

In Port-Louis every façade tells its story. Remnants of successive civilisations that have invaded and left their mark are easily recognisible: the British racecourse; eighteenth-century French squares; Oriental boutiques, African markets and Chinese casinos; temples, mosques and cathedrals; winding lanes and wide avenues lined with palm trees; wrought-iron balconies, their windows and shutters open or shut according to the breeze, heat, light or desire for privacy of the occupants... Port-Louis is an old city made up of this and that, a place where it is pleasant to stroll in the cool of the evening when the crowds of commuters have left for home.

## THE FATE OF THE DODO

Little time remains, however. Port-Louis is surrendering its character to an advancing army of bulldozers and concrete mixers. As Levi-Strauss said, "Mankind is creating a mass civilisation, it is settling down into a monoculture"; even in this remote land of sugar cane the march towards uniformity is already taking its toll. Gone with the wind are our childhood fantasies

*Above: The central railway station, Port-Louis (photo 1901).*

37

and dreams. "Brick upon brick I'll get my block," rings an African nursery rhyme, a refrain that often comes to haunt my mind.

Mauritius is burying her soul in a concrete vault. Anyone can build anything — anywhere. The magic of this little island, this fairyland where Malcolm de Chazal breathed life into the mountains, is fading and giving way to stereotyped tower blocks typical of any European suburb. As Mauritius is developed, it slowly loses its identity: that special *je ne sais quoi*, those elusive elements that composed its charm. Lagoons, mountains, forests, sugar cane fields and wooden houses are being eaten up by apartment blocks, by factories and by land division. Is it really necessary for progress to eliminate systematically the history, variety and individuality of a country?

Singapore's remedy (late but effective) has proved that it is possible to reconcile development with architectural heritage and that the past does offer assets for the future. "Architecture should read like a book": there is no need to tear out the first pages in order to write the following ones. Recent achievements by some Mauritian architects have shown that, after all, it is possible to incorporate old and new into a harmonious blend.

The government, for its part, has begun to realise that it might be detrimental to pile up

storey upon storey — like noughts upon a balance sheet. It recently vetoed the construction of a skyscraper in Port-Louis which would have razed to the ground an eighteenth century building on the famous Place d'Armes.

Perhaps the wooden houses of Mauritius will escape the fate of the dodo (*Didus ineptus*), that large turkey-like bird with atrophied wings whose survival (until the arrival of the Dutch in 1598) exemplified Darwin's theories, but whose disappearance and posthumous fame now only provide copy for tourist brochures. Yet, in the words of Malcolm de Chazal, "To resign oneself is to consign hope to the deep-freeze."

Christian Saglio

*The interior of Le Réduit betrays the comfortable existence of its owners.*

*A typical house in Curepipe displays many traditional architectural features (photo 1953).*

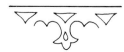

# POPULAR DWELLINGS

The creativity and inspiration behind these houses is equalled only by their apparent joie-de-vivre. Flaunting the conventions of traditional architecture, their riotous colours and abundant decoration are a feast for the eyes. The care with which they were built is a reflection of the pride of the multi-cultural community of Mauritius in their homes: Mauritian style is not difficult to achieve assuming one is willing simply to try.

Up until the 1930s the majority of agricultural and factory workers lived in *cases* as primitive as those of the settlers of the eighteenth century. Most of their houses were built of uncut stone or wattle-and-daub covered with a straw roof. Corrugated iron and brightly-coloured paint — features which now characterise the popular dwelling — date from the 1930s when an increased number of agricultural workers became land owners.

The houses are an adaptation of the existing style of traditional architecture employed by all Mauritians, irrespective of their cultural background. The popular dwelling is a colourful, asymmetric version of the larger house to which a profusion of decoration has been added.

The kitchen is a small separate structure at the rear of the house, situated in a compound amongst the chicken coops, where the smoky smell of burning wood mingles with the sharp odour of spices crushed on the *roche carri*.

The pride with which the owner looks after his house can be detected in its neat and well-kept interior and its brilliantly polished red floor, known locally as a *châlis*. The walls are covered with a multitude of memorabilia but pride of place is always given to religious images.

In Mauritius even the small houses generally have an impressive garden for, climate permitting, Mauritians tend to live outside, or on the verandah, rather than in the house. However tiny, the garden is as picturesque as the house. Unlike their dignified formal counterparts on the plateau or the plantation, these gardens are a jumble of flowers and fruit trees, vegetables and medicinal herbs, a taste of the infinite colour and variety of tropical flora.

Page 40: *This house nestles amidst dense greenery at the foot of the mountains. One can almost feel the coolness of the air and hear the cock crow.*
Left: *Worn by the passage of time, this house is so in keeping with its surroundings that it appears to have grown out of the ground.*
Right: *These popular dwellings form an intrinsic part of the traditional architecture which gives Mauritius its character. It is to be hoped that they will become a source of inspiration for contemporary buildings.*

*Although the architecture of his house follows a certain pattern of rules, every individual is his own architect. Each house is the expression of his creative spirit, although, generally a certain number of established rules are respected. The house is raised off the ground; its roof or roofs are sloping (and often made of corrugated iron); its gables are ventilated by a small slatted window; for the openings, there are two alternatives: either the doors and windows open directly onto the interior, protected by corrugated iron canopies and wooden shutters, or there is a verandah, enclosed by small-paned windows.*

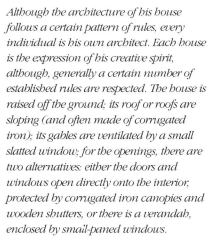

Above: *Owners whose houses look straight onto the street have devised ingenious ways of shielding themselves from the intrusive eyes of passers-by. In this house small wooden panels cover the lower part of the windows.*

Above right: *The style of these dwellings confirms that traditional architecture is not limited to the large wooden residences built by plantation owners.*

Right: *The glazed verandah, however modest, can be a source of inspiration for the revival of modern architecture. It is possible to manufacture on a large scale, reproducing traditional details and using metal instead of wood.*

Above: *Although popular dwellings are usually rural, there are many examples of colourful popular boutiques, such as this one in Floréal. Traditional architecture often features later additions that blend with elegance into the existing structure. Here the living quarters are more recent than the shop below.*

Left: *Simplicity in a verandah often betrays the fact that it is modern. This may be a matter of taste or it may be due to a lack of skilled craftsmen. With the encroaching tide of concrete in Mauritius it is true that many of the crafts traditionally passed from father to son have been lost. Nowadays, however, there is a glimmer of a revival of old-fashioned trades.*

Above: *Traditional architecture often displays a surprising simplicity and lack of decorative detail in its design.*
Right: *The popular dwelling is usually set in a well-kept garden, a reflection of the care and pride of the owner.*

Above: *A juxtapostion of startling colours produces a boldly patterned tableau of naïve art.*
Right: *The most touching dwellings are family houses whose simplicity lends richness.*

Above: *It would seem that an artist used all the tints and hues of his palette to compose this picture.*

Left: *Timber shingles are sometimes used to cover the walls of houses.*

Every facade is unique in its detail. The decorative trim of the verandah and the canopy, the contours of the window surrounds, and the finials are charming examples of local craftsmanship.

# PLANTATION HOUSES

We are in nineteenth century Mauritius, silver cane flowers shimmering against a clear blue sky and the sweet smell of sugar hanging heavy in the air. A tall factory chimney billows clouds of smoke, and all around is a bustle of activity. Beyond, in an arbour of greenery, is the house, noble and majestic, the abode of the planter.

Times have changed but traditions remain. Today, Mauritius still lives to the rhythm of the sugar industry, and most of the houses that were built with the factories have been jealously preserved. The plantation manager generally enjoys the privilege of the house for the duration of his duties.

They can be seen all over the island, wherever sugar cane cultivation provoked the construction of factories. Unfortunately all that now remains of most factories is the large store chimney. Up until 1860 as many as two hundred and sixty plantations existed, but the grand plantation houses were found only on the larger plantations. As years went by plantations were annexed, and there are now only nineteen sugar factories in Mauritius.

It is difficult to define the style of the plantation house. Nowhere are the differences in appearance so marked whilst yet remaining within the traditional mould. There are houses with two storeys and houses with only one, houses with turrets and those with circular verandahs. But despite their many differences they are united by their size and their lack of elaborate detail.

The interiors are usually as grand and large in scale as the house itself. Spacious and airy reception rooms are opulently furnished with imposing sideboards, dining tables for twenty people or more, and elegant chairs and sofas.

The magnificent grounds with century-old trees and vast expanses of lawn add a further dimension to these sumptuous dwellings.

Page 52 and left: *La Villebague owes its name to the estate of La Villebague in St Méloir des Ondes, to the east of St Malo in Brittany. The plantation started producing sugar in 1743, one of the first to do so. The house was built around 1759 by the French governor René Magon who took as his model the Governor's Palace in Pondicherry. The turrets were added in 1934, completely changing the aspect of what was previously a manor house typical of eighteenth-century France. Usually turrets feature only on houses with one storey, but La Villebague is an exception.*
Above: *The verandahs of large houses are often paved with stone.*
Right: *Strong sunlight projects a distorted image of a rattan sofa.*

Beau Sejour is situated at the end of a long avenue of royal palm trees, a surprisingly French approach to a house that was originally built by the British. Originally built by the Anglo-Ceylon Company around 1890, Beau Sejour was rebuilt in 1920, using concrete for the walls and joists. The use of timber for the roof and floors ensured that the charm of this large house was preserved.

*Rays of sun transform this simple fountain at Beau Sejour into a shower of light. Overleaf: Bel Air St Felix was built in the second half of the nineteenth century by the great-grandfather of the present owner who acquired the sugar plantation in 1850. These photographs depict the two dimensions of life on the verandah: the area at the front, with its elegant cane furniture and pot plants, is the place where guests are entertained, and the family domain, within the privacy of the glazed verandah, is at the back. Doors open on each axis, allowing the gentle sea breeze to circulate through the house.*

Left: *In the 1880s Mauricia belonged to an English gentleman whose favourite pastime was growing sweet-peas. Their exquisite aroma was a joy for all those who came to the property. The house was demolished by cyclone Carol in 1960 and subsequently rebuilt on the existing foundations, retaining its old world atmosphere.*

Above: *The formality of the gardens of Mauricia is accentuated by their surroundings— a sea of sugar cane fields on all four sides.*

63

Pages 62-63: *Built at Plaisance around 1870 this house was demolished and rebuilt at Riche-en-Eau in 1890. The new owner transformed it from a two-storey into a single-storey house and introduced the idea of double columns. The gardens reflect the French character of their creator Mr Rochecouste, with their formal lawns, large pools, well-kept alleyways and topiary. An old stone arch covered in greenery greets the visitor at the entrance.*

Far left: *This property was purchased by an Indian in 1898. Although he never came to Mauritius he sent emissaries to build the grand house known as Bel Ombre. It was designed by an architect who was also responsable for the construction of several public buildings in Port-Louis.*

Above and left: *Louvres and raffia blinds of Bel Ombre filter out the strength of the sun.*

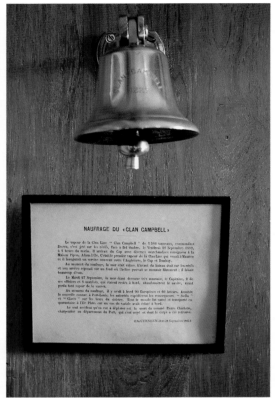

Above: *This bell was salvaged from the wreck of the Clan Campbell, the first steam boat of the Clan line to come to Mauritius. It met its fate on the reef opposite Bel Ombre in September 1882.*

Left and right: *Much of the furniture of Bel Ombre was rescued from the Rouillard residence in Curepipe when it was demolished. Originally all of the glass in the doors was coloured.*

Left: *Labourdonnais remains one of the few houses built according to strictly-defined plans under the supervision of a French architect (M. Rampant). Work started in 1856 and was completed in 1858.*
Above: *The French windows of the pavilion, built in 1910. "It was not uncommon here in this island for three or four sons or sons-in-law with their wives and families to live in their own pavilions on the old people's estate, meeting at breakfast and dinner around the family table." (Bengal Civilian, 1835)*

"In that land of the sun, the purity of the atmosphere, the rich and magical lines of colour, the softness of the aerial perspective, the powerful relief of light and shadows produce impressions of pleasure rarely equalled even in our finest days..." (Frederic Mouat). Simple and majestic, this verandah derives its style from its imposing dimensions and from its harmony of form and tone. Before wickerwork became fashionable at the beginning of this century the furniture on the verandah was much the same as in the sitting room: armchairs, sofas and cane-bottomed chairs.

Above: *This magnificent avenue of Chinese banyan trees (*Ficus retusa*) was planted around 1820. It is very likely that it led to the house that existed previously on the site of Labourdonnais.*

Right: *The wrought-iron balustrade of Labourdonnais is one of the finest on the island.*

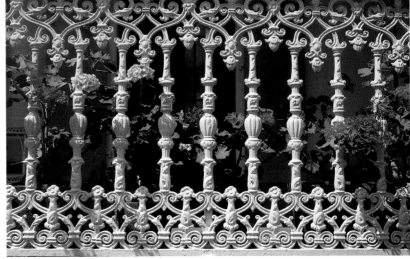

Above: *In this ancestral home every suite of furniture has its story; and every story is irrevocably entangled with the past. Rarely would a Mauritian home have displayed features as sophisticated as these: the tapestry, the chandelier, the panelled doors and the French parquet flooring are signs of the original occupants' close contacts with their homeland.*

Left: *In his* Rambles around Mauritius *of 1855, Mr Clark refers to the well-maintained kitchen garden and its delicious fruit and vegetables.*

The furniture in the dining room and the study was bought by Henry Barlow during on of his voyages to London in the 1850s. The tapestry, ordered in 1906 to replace the original one, was made in Alsace.

Overleaf: The Burke Hotel was built in 1840, a rustic structure, probably thatched, on the road to Forest Side. It was destroyed by a cyclone in 1872. The existing house, known as Les Aubineaux, was built by M. Bestel. Its numerous embellishments, notably the turrets, were added at a later date by the Rochecouste and the Guimbeau families.

74

# PLATEAU
# HOUSES

Hidden hither and thither along the winding roads which criss-cross the upper plateau, these houses come in all shapes and sizes.

Towards the end of the nineteenth century, two simultaneous influences — a malaria epidemic and the expansion of the railways — encouraged the expansion of this region. The malaria epidemic was so devastating that many Mauritians moved from the low-lying Pamplemousses and Port-Louis area to the plateau where the climate was supposed to be more salubrious. For a long time, Moka was the place to be. Villas sprung up along the main road which hugs the mountain range. A few families have remained faithful to this area, but most moved to the Plaines Wilhems as more facilities became available in the towns on the central railway line. As the railways were extended, office workers began to commute to Port-Louis and so the trend to move was further encouraged.

French nineteenth-century architecture was traditionalist in comparison with the British taste for the picturesque: the charm of the plateau house lies in its combination of both these tendencies.

Its variety of silhouettes contrasts with the simple shape of the early nineteenth-century house. The purity of the earlier form was enriched by new elements — a multitude of roof shapes, turrets, glazed verandahs, bow-windows, auvents — all of which created endless imaginative possibilities.

Despite the variety of forms, one can distinguish four broad categories in this region: houses with simple large columns; those with a colonnade and balustrade; those with turrets; and those with glazed verandahs. Of course some houses belong to more than one category. Plateau houses basically being suburban dwellings, the size of the garden usually reflects the size of the house: large houses have large gardens; small houses have small gardens.

Far left: *Eureka at Moka has been a museum since 1986 and is the only Mauritian house complete with period furniture that is open to the public. With its 14 rooms and 109 doors and windows, it is the largest house on the island. It was built in 1830 by Mr Carr, an eminent Scot who wanted to live in close proximity to the Governor's residence at La Réduit. From 1856 to 1986 it was the home of the Leclezio family.*

Left: *This cast-iron four-poster bed is a rare sight on the island of Mauritius.*

Below: *The bathroom houses a collection of period pieces: an old-fashioned shower, a hip-bath and a washstand with its pitcher and basin. Cut from a single block of marble and weighing over 500 kilograms the bath is unique. It originates from India and was ordered in the eighteenth century by Mr Chintamun Gujadhur, a distinguished gentleman of Indian origin. Above the bath is an example of a wood-fuelled water heater.*

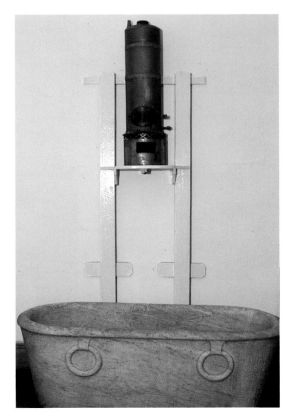

Champrosay was built by an Englishman around 1850. It was acquired by the avid collector Mr Lois Le Vieux in 1967. The verandah exudes a typical aura of relaxation and well-being.

The formal sitting room. When Champrosay was purchased this room was divided by a partition and the door on the right had been done away with. During restoration work the door was rediscovered in the cellar and was immediately reinstated. The chandelier and the gilded bronze clock were originally in Valory, a large residence in Moka. The central table is probably an early nineteenth century British piece, of a style known locally as "East India Company". The cabinet on the left is thought to be an authentic Boulle; it is interesting to note that Mr Le Vieux discovered an identical cabinet in the Wallace Collection in London.

*The study. On the wall above the desk
(another "East India Company" piece)
hangs a hand-embroidered tapestry
depicting Van Dyck and Rembrandt. It is
the work of the young ladies boarding at
Madame Benoit's academy in 1860. The
bronze statue of the god Pan is by Coysevox
and dates from 1769.*

Left: *In a country where one lives in close proximity with nature, it is often impossible to draw the line between house and garden. Here the house seems to be an extension of its garden.*

Above and right: *Against a back-drop of blue sky the symmetrical composition of the house is a successful synthesis of turrets, glazed verandah, window overhangs, dormer windows and decorative detailing.*

The play of light and shade on the verandah creates a strange graphic composition. *"These houses were conceived and constructed at a time when daring and invention were in direct proportion to man's imagination. They exalt the knowledge of the forest ranger, the logcutter, the master sawyer and the squarer, as well as the skill of artisans of various trades: the stone-hewer, the mason, the smelter, the smith, the cabinet-maker, the joiner, the ironworker, the tinsmith, the turner and the carpenter..."* (Raymond Chasle, Maisons Traditionelles de l'Ile Maurice)

Above: *Unlike the open verandah with its modest and easily movable furniture, the glazed verandah is protected from the vicissitudes of the elements. Its atmosphere is cosy and it lends itself easily to use as a sitting room.*

Right: *This house in Quatre Bornes has belonged to the Moolan family since 1941. The glazed verandah was completely replaced and redecorated in 1950. The woodwork is as fine as lace.*

Left: *Béthanie at Beau-Bassin. Its architecture expresses a strong love of sobriety and elegance.*

Right: *This house on Shand Street, Beau-Bassin, was constructed during the late nineteenth century.*

Above: *Verdun dates from the first years of the twentieth century and has remained the property of the Dawood family since 1940. The bow windows were added around 1950. Although the glazing has suffered from many cyclones, the owners have always felt honour-bound to replace it.*

Left: *The varangue at Les Palmiers at Phoenix is laid with traditional stone paving cut from the basalt rock that is found all over the island.*

Above and right: *The timeless and peaceful quality of the verandah at Béthanie is inspired as much by the simple detailing of the columns and balustrade as by the delicacy of the plants and the sophistication of the furniture.*

Above: *The porch and bow window of Les Palmiers, Phoenix, betray the influence of the British on the architecture of this late ninteenth century house.*

Left: *The outhouses have been converted into a pavilion where guests and relatives can stay.*

"Coffee on the verandah, a deliciously fresh air and bright moonlight; there are moments that repay one for a tropical midday; the evening and the early morning are divine and to see the people sitting listlessly in their deep chairs giving themselves up entirely to the soft languor that then creeps over one, you would think them the most careless beings on earth, as in one sense, perhaps, they are...". The comments of the Bengal Civilian, made in his journal of 1838, are just as applicable to life on the verandah today.

91

Les Quatre Vents in Moka, with its whitewashed walls, black roof, Wedgewood-blue shutters, long, square-columned verandah and tall French windows, represents all that is most typical of traditional Mauritian architecture. The colours — white, black and Wedgewood blue — were not chosen at random but because they are the colours that were used in the early days of building. Roofs used to be covered in the black bitumen paint used by naval boatbuilders to protect the hulls; walls were whitewashed with lime produced locally by burning madrepores; and the blue of the shutters was achieved by adding permanganate (to protect the wood from termites) to this lime.

Left: *This house on Shand Street, Beau-Bassin, is practically enveloped by a flowering mango tree and a cascade of bougainvillea.*

Right: *Strong sunlight creates a dramatic pattern of white against a dark background. This might explain why decorative detailing is found mostly on the verandah. "There is, when the blinds are down, a bird-cage look about them..." (C S Boyle,* Far Away, or Sketches of Scenery and Society in Mauritius, *1867)*

Headquarters House in Vacoas was built in 1870 by Edmond de Chazal and now belongs to the government. It owes its British colonial look to extensive additions made in 1904. The porch, crowned with a turret, dates from this time. It also has a surprising resemblance to the architecture of certain Caribbean islands. The chimney might seem out of place in a tropical country but in fact it does serve a function in "the highlands" where winter temperatures often fall to 10°C and humidity is high.

Chateau Trompette in Moka was built
around 1870 by Mr Janvier Desvaux and
was named after the house of the same
name in Bordeaux. A British general
rented the house in the 1890s and is said to
have given grand balls to the rousing
sound of military bands. Mr Montocchio
who lived in La Malmaison (now the
Curepipe Town Hall) moved to Trompette
in 1894 with his family of nine children.

*"It had those tall doors, half-door and half-window, veiled by muslin curtains with those impossble ornate handles working on rods that you find in French houses. They opened out of all the rooms in all directions and led into all the other rooms." (F. D. Ommaney,* The Shoals of Capricorn, *1952)*

The dining room. The huge table used to be laid for the 18 members of the Montocchio family. The brass candelabra was acquired in Europe at the turn of the century. Being extremely farsighted, the owner of the house acquired a duplicate of its opal globe at the same time, and also bought a second, identical tapestry for the drawing room.

The glazed verandah was probably adopted in Mauritius as an extension of the trend for conservatories and glasshouses which spread throughout Europe in the nineteenth century. This type of verandah is a phenonomen particular to the architecture of Mauritius; it is interesting to note that it is rarely seen in other countries that otherwise have a similar style of architecture. On Mauritius, roughly one in three houses have a glazed verandah. They look as if they are hermetically sealed, but, in fact, the small panes can often be opened to ensure a constant flow of air during the summer. These small panes are also able to resist the force of cyclones, whereas large glass windows are fragile and can be dangerous.

Left: *This house in Curepipe exudes an atmosphere of romance despite its worn appearance.*

Above: *Children seem to discover the world leaning out of the window.*

There are some houses whose roofs are of corrugated iron but whose turrets are shingled. Perhaps this is because shingles last longer on steeper roofs? The desire to catch the eye of the passer-by brought more and more decorative detailing to houses on the street. Dormer windows on turrets often had no other function than to embellish the façade of a house. Wood had to be painted so that it would resist bad weather and, often, as in the case of these French windows, it was veined to imitate the natural wood which was so fashionable in Europe during the early years of the twentieth century.

As years went by the smaller houses endeavoured to emulate their forebears, imitating their elegance, their serenity and even the proud dignity of their turrets. The French window was common in modest dwellings as well as grand houses. When the summer heat becomes stifling the openings, always placed opposite each other on the same axis, allow the air to circulate and provide refreshing ventilation.

Sorèze House in Vacoas owes its name to the property of that name at Les Pailles where the house was originally built. It was moved to its present location at the end of the nineteenth century. The large round columns stand like sentinels on the bare verandah of the house.

Above: *"The polished floor, beautiful to look at but dangerous to the equilibrium of the uninitiated..." (Rev. Beaton,* Creoles and Coolies or Five Years in the Mauritius, *1859)*

Right: *Note that some of the windows at Sorèze House do not descend to the floor; this affords a better use of space within the house. Although French windows provide ventilation they may, if numerous, make for difficulties in arranging furniture.*

Left: *This unusual house, probably built around the end of the nineteenth century, exemplified all the genius of Mauritian craftsmen. It was one of the most intensely decorated houses on the plateau, but was demolished in 1998.*

Above and right: *La Sablonnière in Curepipe was built around 1888 by Mr de Chazal. He named it after a family property in Auvergne. The Eiffel Tower in the garden is an exact replica of the Parisian Eiffel Tower and was erected in 1889.*

Overleaf: *These photographs demonstrate the diversity of styles found in the houses of the plateau. Large or small, the options are endless: open or glazed verandahs, hipped or gabled roofs, dormer windows or turrets, one storey or more…*

Left: *During the last decade the façade of this house in Petit Raffray was rebuilt using concrete, but retaining the original roof and turrets. The result is a startling, although not entirely unsuccessful, mixture of styles.*

Below left: *The painter's brush was all that was needed to give this house a new lease of life.*

*"What joy it must have been to see the canopies installed, the roof go up, the shingles nailed down, and the decorative trim of the verandah put in its place to balance the rigour of the roof structure...".* (Raymond Chasle, Maisons Traditionelles de l'Ile Maurice)

Overleaf: *La Rocherie in Rose Hill was probably built at the end of the nineteenth century. The foundations are built of the same stone as the local church, Notre Dame de Lourdes. Julie Comtesse de Carne lived here for many years before her death in 1986 at the age of 103.*

Left: *According to legend, Le Réduit was built in 1748 to be a country house for Barthélemy David. In fact, his plans were further reaching: placed between two ravines, the house would serve as a refuge in case of attack by the English. In this very same year, General Boscowan attempted to take the island by surprise and David's work was justified. However, the original wooden building soon fell into disrepair and was rebuilt in stone in 1778 by le Chevalier Guiran de la Brillane. It is currently the home of the president of the Republic.*

Above: *The Temple d'Amour was built by Sir Hesketh Bell (governor from 1916 to 1924) in memory of Barthélemy David.*

Left: *The eye floats gently over the garden to the Bout du Monde, a breathtaking viewpoint overlooking steep ravines.*
Above: *The rear verandah of Le Réduit is bathed in the golden light of sunset. This house has been compared to a small-scale, tropical Versailles.*
Overleaf: *This house in Vacoas belongs to the Rajcoomar family. It was built by an English sea captain. The house differs from most traditional architecture due to its central corridor; the owner wished to recreate the atmosphere of a ship's galley.*

When the British forces first arrived in Mauritius in 1810 they built their army barracks on the coast. They were moved from here to Curepipe in 1875 and thence to Vacoas in 1903 as a consequence of the typhoid epidemic of 1890. These buildings are now occupied by the Special Mobile Forces of Mauritius. The roof is unusual: instead of the usual shingles, it is covered with asbestos tiles, specially imported from England.

Overleaf: *Curepipe Town Hall, before renovation. The beautiful house of La Malmaison was originally built at St Pierre in 1790. At the end of the nineteenth century the house was sold, demolished and rebuilt at Curepipe where the original plan was substantially modified but the original timbers were reused. The new building was inaugurated in 1902 and still serves as a "salle des fêtes".*

126

# URBAN ARCHITECTURE

Port-Louis: the capital has always been at the centre of Mauritian life. Originally known as "the Camp", and then as the "Northwest Port", it only became Port-Louis under Labourdonnais. But the name was not final: the town was also known as "Port du Montagne" and, under Decaen an order was passed on 17 August 1906 renaming it "Port Napoleon".

Both capital and commerical centre, Port-Louis' history really began in 1735 with the arrival of Mahé de Labourdonnais. A governor of great genius who combined the roles of architect and engineer, he contrived to build up the town in a very short space of time. However it is to Cossigny, who played his part before the day of Labourdonnais, that we owe the rigour of the town plan established in 1732. The various districts of the town gradually took shape, the size of the grid determining the size of the house. The variety of grid sizes gave the town its well-defined framework of blocks, still in evidence today, and comparable to collection of chessboards of varying sizes.

Most Port-Louis houses are set back from the street in a garden, but there are also small houses built onto the pavement, peculiar only to urban architecture. In the commercial district one comes across boutiques, the ground floor given over to commerce and the first floor to family living.

Towards the end of the nineteenth century urban development began to sprawl out along the roads and railways; today a serpentine development connects Port-Louis and Mahebourg.

Public buildings are usually found within the urban framework. Simple and devoid of decoration they represent a parallel architectural development in Mauritius. Although most homes were built of wood, civil engineers and government officials had greater confidence in stone and this material was generally adopted for all public buildings.

Page 128: *The façade of this office building in Port-Louis is exceptionally austere, with its stonework, heavy door and wrought-iron balustrade.*

Left: *Government House was one of the first buildings to be built by Mahé de Labourdonnais on his arrival in Mauritius in 1735. The second storey was added in 1809 by General Decaen, the last French governor of the island. It has been the seat of successive governments: French, British and, since 1968, Mauritian.*

Above: *Bowen Square, Port-Louis. A fountain dating from 1915 stands in front of the Ireland Blyth building. During 1989, the Year of the Environment, this square was totally renovated.*

Above: *This detail illustrates features typical of most public buildings in Port-Louis. Built of stone it has wooden shutters, a wrought iron balustrade and decorative trimmings in both metal and wood.*
Right: *Construction of the Mauritius Institute or Port-Louis Museum commenced on 23 November 1880; Governor Bowen laid the first stone. Nowadays it houses a natural history collection, an art gallery and a library.*
Overleaf: *The Flacq Court buildings were built by Governor Archibald Gordon (governor from 1871 to 1874). The architectural design was inspired by his castle in Scotland.*

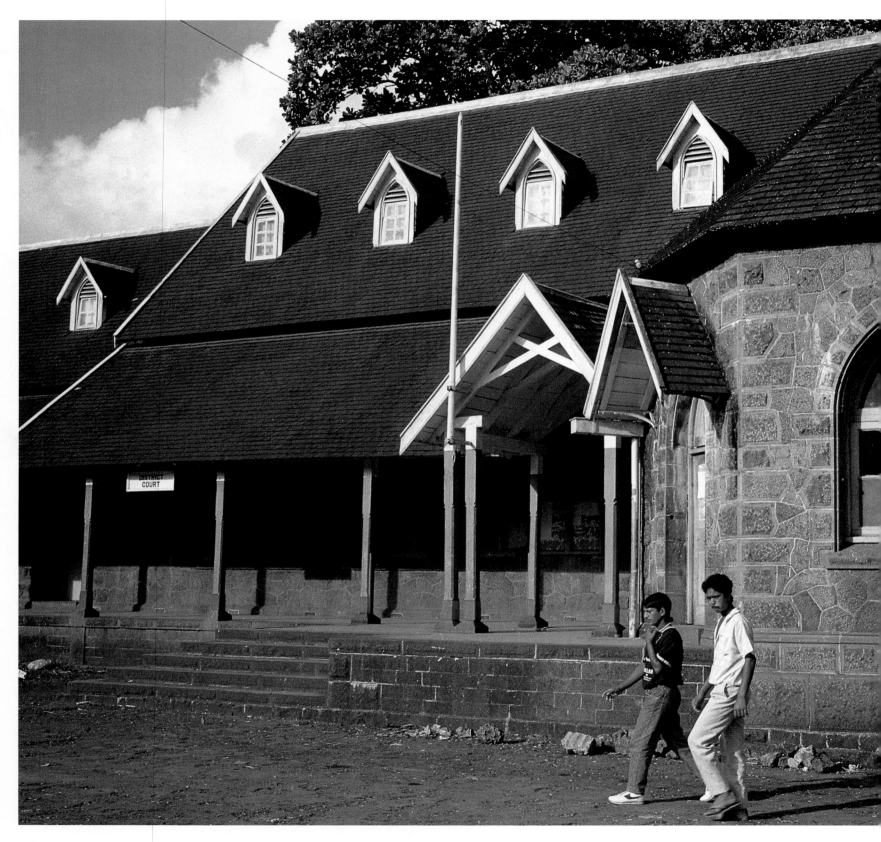

Above: *This building has been saved from demolition and is now used as offices. Built around 1857 it was the residence of Thomy Thiery until his return to France in 1875. An avid collector, this Mauritian was made Chevalier de la Legion d'Honneur for his work in safeguarding many French treasures. On his death his important collection of works of art went to the Louvre.*
Left: *The cast-iron columns of the verandah are ingeniously designed to serve as rainwater pipes.*

*Built around 1823, this house has belonged to the parish of the Immaculate Conception since 1866. Note the balustrade made of oak staves and the old lamp posts that support the pergola. "This building was constructed to resist cyclones as ship resists hurricanes..." (Father Henri Souchon, Vicar of the Immaculate Conception).*

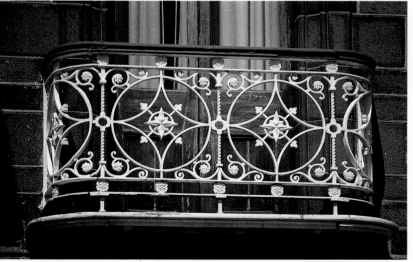

Above: *Mon Désir in Port-Louis has resisted the ravages of the humid climate, losing none of its nobility and antiquated charm.*
Left: *The balcony of the Ireland Blyth building in Port-Louis displays typical evidence of the skill of local artisans.*

Right: *As early as 1812 Milbert mentioned the Mauritian practice of converting attic space in gable ends into bedrooms. He also noted that people in the tropics preferred wooden houses to more solid constructions: "Experience has taught them that this kind of building is better suited to the climate. Wood does not conduct heat, allowing it to penetrate only slowly and deflecting most of the light."*

Below right: *"In wood there are latent shapes that can be awakened by the artisan's tool. It is a warm and vibrant material that can become the spirit of a home, and no manmade product will ever replace it. Wood talks and sings and works; it has a presence of its own." (Bernard Clavel).*

Mon Rêve, residence of Mlle Adèle, was built before the cyclone of 1892. It was bought by Mr Adèle, the father of the present owner, in 1911. It was he who closed the verandah on both sides, built the wall and gate and, in 1925, added a second storey.

Above: *The famous Wedgewood blue, so loved by Mauritians, has been used to decorate the interior of this bedroom.*
Left: *Often seen on the verandah, the polished red floor — or châlis — probably originates from India. In more modest abodes this style of floor may be adopted throughout the house.*

Since the death of Mlle Adèle's mother, almost fifty years ago, this room has remained unchanged. All of the furniture was ordered by her father in 1908 and made by a Mauritian joiner, Mr Sandivi. His workshop used to be next to the theatre in Port-Louis.

Above: *The bedroom is a repository for religious icons and all kinds of family memorabilia, the kind of room that is "reminiscent of the white walls of the seminary and the mass..."* (Loys Masson, Les autres nourritures).

Left: *The terracotta statue representing the muse Sapho was purchased by Mlle Adèle's father on a trip to France.*

143

Above: *Town houses are usually set in walled gardens or courtyards amongst large trees that provide ample shade. Yet space is still at a premium. Whilst people living in the highlands could easily extend their houses by adding a wing to the side or the back, the people of Port-Louis had only one option: to convert the roof. The design is always simple, providing a comfortable living area within.*

Left: *This balcony, originally looking straight onto the road in Port-Louis, has been enclosed with glass.*

*On 6 June 1769, the day of his arrival in Mauritius, then the Ile de France, Mr Desroches (governor from 1769 to 1772) made the first proclamation regarding the appearance of the capital. Inhabitants were hitherto obliged to enclose their house or land with a wall or, failing that, with a living hedge of bamboo, acacia, or other prickly bush. Fences made of palisades, planks or any other kind of dead wood were forbidden. Every owner should plant on his land eleven trees, such as tamarind, mango or peach trees, at intervals that were prescribed according to the acreage of the land in question. According to Governor Desroches, a place as hot as the town of Port-Louis, denuded of greenery for most of the year, produced a sad and unattractive impression (A Toussaint,* Port-Louis: deux siècles d'histoire*).*

These small urban houses are built right on the pavement are typical of Port-Louis. This simple style of architecture has long been in existence and has often been depicted in old prints and engravings.

*"Yoloffs Street". The name of this street is not fortuitous: it has definite historical origins. In the days of French rule the town of Port-Louis was divided into three sections: the town centre, the western district and the eastern district. One of the areas within the eastern district was known as "Camp Yoloff" because it was the home of the descendants of the Yoloffs from Senegal.*

Left: *Modern day Port-Louis has been invaded by motorcycles, lorries and cars, and yet handcarts are still used to transport merchandise.*

Right: *Two-storey boutiques, such as this one in Beau Bassin, are sometimes found outside Port-Louis. The shop is on the ground floor and the family lives above.*

Below right: *Corrugated iron is often used on walls instead of wooden planks.*

The "boutique", equivalent to the corner shop, is found all over the island of Mauritius. Its merchandise varies according to the means of the owner and to its location. Some boutiques only sell the bare necessities whilst others have an amazingly colourful profusion of disparate wares, worthy of an Ali Baba's cave. As well as pots of jam, there are babies' bottles and dominos, plaster models of the well-loved Father Laval (priest of Mauritius) and coconut brooms, and all the usual small goods of the ironmonger, such as nails and glue... The boutique will allow the customer to buy in bulk or on credit but it is also a place where you can by a single cigarette, a candle or a sardine sandwich.

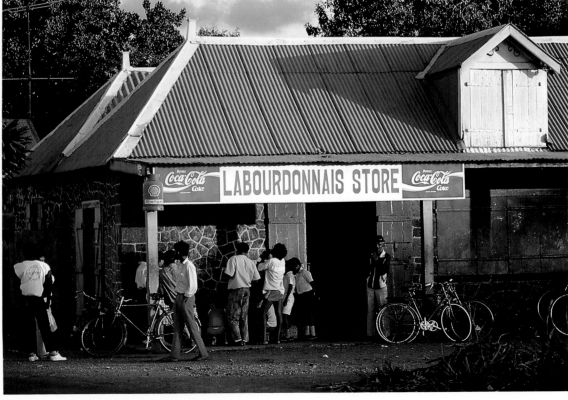

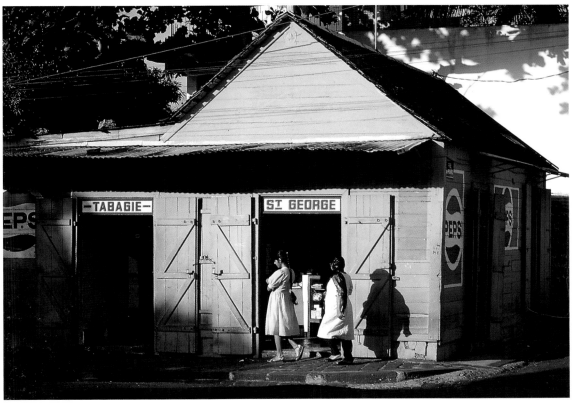

*The boutique is at the heart of Mauritian daily life. It is a social place where men gather while the women look after the home. Outside the boutique street vendors gather to sell their pistachios, spicy sweets, samosas and other snacks, knowing that here they have a guaranteed market for their wares.*

*The magnificent Episcopal Palace is the creation of master builders Darode and Gilbert. Its construction was a major project: work started in April 1847 and lasted until October 1852.*

*This is a typical commercial boutique in Port-Louis, characterised by colourful walls and shutters. Sadly, unless demolition and redevelopment are controlled, buildings such as this are doomed.*

*Poncini, the well-known Port-Louis store,
has held out steadfastly against the concrete
invasion. The startlingly Parisian street
lamp in the foreground was a replacement
for the miniature Eiffel Tower (presented at
the Universal Exhibition of Paris in 1889)
which stood here before being moved to
La Sablonnière at Curepipe.*

Although no-one knows the exact date of
construction of this building on the Place
des Armes, Port-Louis, records show that the
Oriental Banking Corporation operated
here during the years between 1852 and
1885. It is now the premises of the Hong
Kong Bank. The red-roofed building in the
background dates from the very first years
of the French colony on Mauritius. Once
the bakery that provided bread and biscuits
for fleets en route to the West Indies, it
became the home of the national mint. The
building was demolished in 1990.

155

These houses at the Champ de Mars in
Port-Louis are perched on the hillsides
surrounded by the mountain range of
Port-Louis.
It would be logical to associate the glazed
verandah with the central plateau where
the climate is cooler and more humid,
but these two houses demonstrate that the
glazed verandah is in fact a social
phenomenon rather than a utilitarian
development.

# 'CAMPEMENTS'
# AND HOTELS

The rustle of the filaos trees, the lapping of the waves… here, in the most perfect surroundings, one comes across the *campement* made of ravenala with its roof of straw, symbol of a bygone age.

The joys of the coast were discovered at the turn of the century when the eradication of malaria and the arrival of the motorcar combined to stimulate development in areas previously inaccessible and considered to be insalubrious. Mauritians began to spend the winter months in rudimentary dwellings known as "campements". They used to bring almost all household goods for the "season", this giving birth to the expression "going camping".

A whole generation of Mauritians still remembers the palava of setting off. Under the vigilant eye of the mistress of the house the ox-drawn carts are numbered and their contents listed: chairs, mattresses, small pieces of furniture, kitchen implements and clothing, not forgetting the chicken coops. The convoy moves off at about eight o'clock and heads for the coast. Soon afterwards the members of the family, who have been ready for hours, pile into the

car to follow. Children crave for that first heady smell of the sea. The car will reach its destination first, and only when, late in the afternoon, the carts finally arrive, has the season truly begun.

In the post-war period Mauritian traditional architecture disappeared, and the experience of nearly two centuries of tropical living was temporarily forgotten, to be replaced by the modern style. Only in the last 20 years has the Mauritian vernacular, and the verandah's charm, been rediscovered.

The Mauritian style developed primarily to cater for housing needs; its revival however is due to a large extent to the hotel industry which has sought to marry the traditional elements of Mauritian architecture with a contemporary way of life and modern technology. As most hotels are found in coastal regions, it is the old "campement" style which has influenced the materials used; with basalt stone walls and paving, and thatched roofs in "vetiver" and sugar cane. The verandah, which epitomises the Mauritian style, is also present. The influence of the Far East can also be found in many recent hotels.

Page 158: *"We, the children of Mauritius, slumber in a cradle rocked by the waves of the Indian Ocean just within the tropics…"* (*CJ Boyle,* Far Away, or Sketches of Scenery and Society in Mauritius, *1867*).

Above and left: *In 1989, Mauritians celebrated the 350th anniversary of the introduction of deer to the island (8 November 1639). The deer were imported from Indonesia and set free at the foot of the Montagne du Lion. There are accounts by Milbert from as early as 1804 describing hunting parties that lasted for more than a week.*

Above: *The memoirs of the fanatical Alfred Montocchio mention the elation of seeing a trophy, even years after it was taken.*

Above right: *These twining branches are called "liane de cerf". They are often used as balustrades for hunting lodges, or "campements de chasse", as they are known locally.*

Right: *The old oil lamp and copper water tank are vestiges of the days of the primitive, yet comfortable, hunting lodges.*

161

*How many times have these walls heard the story of seven deer killed by seven shots...? A single glance at a trophy will bring back all the memories of where a certain stag was shot and how he fell.*

Above: *The Domaine de Chasseur, opened in 1988, is a park where the public can go shooting or hiking and can even eat and stay the night.*
Right: *This tree fern of the genus* Cyathea, *known locally as "fandia", is a protected species.*

Above: *La Hutte in Trou d'Eau Douce was built in 1906 by Henri Leclezio , the owner of Euréka. Destroyed by cyclone Carol in 1960, it was subsequently rebuilt on its existing foundations.*

Left: *The construction of the roof is visible from the inside. The thatch is attached to the wood-and-bamboo structure with rope made of coconut fibres.*

Right: *A contemporary extension has been added to a traditional campement: the walls are of concrete but the roof is of ravenala. The glazed verandah serves as a corridor between the two parts of the house, protecting the inmates from the strong trade winds.*

Below right: *Many of the traditional campements on the east coast of the island have no verandah on the seaward side as it is uncomfortable to sit outside during the winter months. The casuarina trees, known locally as "filaos", form an integral part of the seaside landscape.*

Left: *In contrast to the usual light rattan furniture of the verandah, this incongruous mixture of objects creates a cosy atmosphere of permanence.*

Above: *Until 1860 when gas was introduced to Mauritius, lamps such as this were fuelled by sperm whale oil.*

Above: *"The mosquito net barely protected me from the greedy hum of mosquitoes..."* (Arthur Martial, Sphinx de Bronze).
Right: *The interior of a campement is often dark due to the use of ravenala, to the stained wooden beams (black varnish prevents termite attack) and to the dark red châlis. Until relatively recently campements were used only as holiday homes and their construction was rudimentary.*

This campement in Trou d'Eau Douce is an invitation to wallow in sweet idleness. It is easy to imagine a family group reclining languidly in deep armchairs in the shade of the broad verandah. Although inadequate in the high humidity of the plateau, thatched roofs often feature amongst houses on the coast. They have to be replaced (assuming that they are not destroyed by a cyclone) every twenty years or so.

Right: *Like the large house on the plantation, the campement may also have its pavilion to accommodate the all the members of large families.*
Below right: *The palm tree, heavy with coconuts, adds the seal of exoticism to the luxuriant tropical garden.*

Ideally situated on the beach, La Maison looks out over the ever-changing hues of the ocean towards the northern islands. Inaugurated at the end of 1987, it is a luxurious and elegant traditional-style villa where people can stay throughout the year. Overleaf: This moorish-style house on the small island known as "l'Ilot Cocos" in Blue Bay was built by Sir Hesketh Bell (governor from 1916 to 1924).

The Oberoi Hotel, Mauritius, is situated
on the northwest coast of the island in
Turtle Bay at Pointe aux Piments. The
architecture has had numerous
influences– Indonesian, Thai, African
and Indian. During construction huge
ochre rocks were found on the site and
have been used in the magnificent
gardens. They influenced the ochre
colours of the buildings.
Page 174: A garden sculpture in front of
one of the villas, a sumptuous mix of
stone, wood and thatch.

Page 175: The Indonesian sculptures (at
top and bottom) are carved from blocks
of stone and were imported. The famous
Dodo immortalized (centre).
Above: The entrance hall and sunset
pavilion dominate a fish pond with a
view out to sea. Between the two
buildings an aqueduct creates a gentle
waterfall. From here the view over the
lagoon is impressive. The sunset pavilion
resembles a watch tower, and was built
specially to sit and watch the setting sun.

Right: The pool with its reclining
sculptures. Unusual ochre columns set
into the sand serve as torches. The view
looks towards Port-Louis with its
mountain range on one side and the
turquoise lagoon on the other.

Pages 178-179: *The Prince Maurice Hotel on the east coast is named after Maurice de Nassau, a Dutch prince at the time of the Dutch occupation of Mauritius in 1598. At sunset, the jade coloured water of the swimming pool reflects the roofs made of sugar cane leaves and the basalt stone of the hotel's architecture.*

Above and left: *The Residence Hotel on the east coast is reminiscent of Mauritian traditional architecture with wooden balustrades, fretwork and columns. On the hotel's verandah, the planters' chairs recall the lifestyle of bygone years.*

*The Royal Palm Hotel in Grand Bay is part of the Beachcomber group. It is built on one of the most magnificent sites on an island originally called Grand Sable. The hotel has been renovated and extended twice to maintain its tradition of opulent comfort. It is a peaceful haven.*

Sun International's Touessrok hotel was named by its original owners who, while touring Europe at the beginning of the last century, visited the island of Tuesroc in Britanny. On their return they named the islet Touessrok. It was then only accessible by boat. The Moorish architecture of the rooms also has a Mauritian touch with its roofs of sugar cane leaves where the smell of thatch lingers.

Above: *The bar at Touessrok overlooks the channel that used to separate the island from the mainland.*

Right: *A bridge now joins the island with the mainland. The rooms enjoy a superb view over the lagoon of Trou d'Eau Douce.*

Right: *Hotel Touessrok.*

Below right: *The Flagship hotel of the Sun International Group, the St Geran is considered to be one of the most beautiful hotels in the world. First impressions are of paramount importance. This was probably what the architect had in mind when he designed the hotel's entrance with this superb view of the sea.*

Left: *The St Geran hotel swimming pool faces the open sea on the east coast where, in 1744, a beautiful sailing ship from the Compagnie des Indes, the St Geran, was wrecked. One of the masterpieces of French romantic literature, Bernadin de St Pierre's* Paul et Virginie *is an imaginary love story based on this authentic shipwreck.*

Bottom left: *This cool and relaxing background is a sanctuary after the dazzling sunlight of the beach.*

The Hilton Hotel in Flic en Flac has been designed in the Indonesian style. Each bungalow bears the name of a local mango tree: Josée, Aristide, Rosa, Baissac. These form three joined semi-circles which contain the hotel's one hundred and ninety rooms, each with a view of the sea.

Left: The gardens were created by a Hawaiian landscape designer. The thatched roofs and wooden footbridges are in harmony with the tropical surroundings: coconut trees, frangipanis, badamiers, casuarinas, la fouches and flame trees. The pools, decorated with basalt rocks, are interlinked and stocked with Koi fish.

Above: The swimming pool and beach bar.

The Sugar Beach is another Sun
International hotel. It is built in the colonial
style and each villa houses ten rooms.
Left: *The lobby where guests are welcomed.
The rattan furniture recreates the typical
atmosphere of the Mauritian verandah.*
Above: *The rum bar: After dinner, guests
can linger here to savour an old local
rum or a selection of cigars from all
over the world.*
Right: *The entrance hall.*

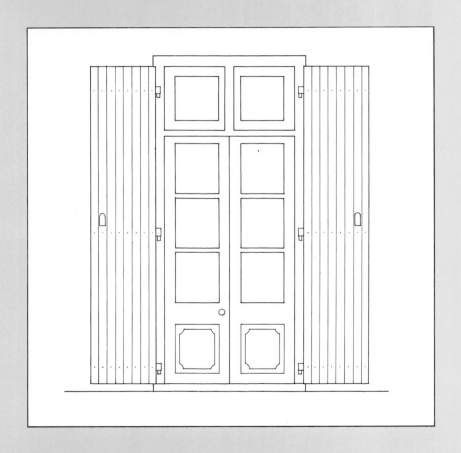

# ARCHITECTURAL NOTEBOOK

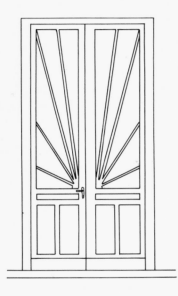

They are in such perfect harmony with their surroundings that one wonders which came first: nature or the houses. Be they large or small, they are a living testimony to a way of life well adapted to the social and climatic conditions of the island. They are unique in the world: a synthesis of all the social and architectural trends that have affected Mauritius over the years of its development.

The sense of magic that emanates from Mauritian traditional architecture evolved slowly from the primitive stone or wooden houses of the first French settlers, each generation providing its contribution. Nobody can state with certainty who exactly contributed those particular features - the verandah, the turrets, the balustrades, the auvents or the decorative ironwork. The cultural and ethnic diversity of the population of Mauritius can be felt intensely in its traditional houses.

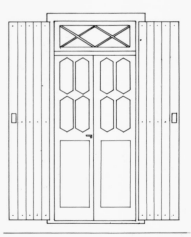

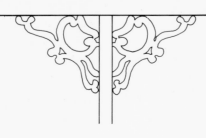

# EARLY DAYS 1715-1820

By the eighteenth century, the Mauritian economy was only just taking shape and the early dwellings were primitive. Mahé de Labourdonnais (governor of the island from 1735 to 1747) tried to persuade the settlers to improve their houses and went as far as providing them with the necessary materials and craftsmen.

The first settlers sought to transplant something of what they had left in France to their new land. Mongoust (demolished in 1912) demonstrated clearly their sentimental attachment to their homeland. Similarly, having abandoned their estates in France, Le Juge de Segrais and his family built a "little Segrais" in Mauritius. But whereas the Château de Segrez was designed by an architect and built by specialist craftsmen, Mongoust was the work of the settlers themselves. "Entirely of wood, this dwelling was a true manor house, a vast rectangular building on two floors... it was sombre in style, with good proportions, it contained no colonial features, and with its large cornice and classical detailing it showed all the

*Built in 1803, demolished in 1912 :
" ...This dwelling was a true manor house, a vast rectangular building on two floors. It was 21 metres long and 15.50 meters wide, built on a high stone podium which surrounded it on all sides. The entrances were approached by two large flights of twelve steps on both the main façades."
René Le Juge de Segrais , in his* Souvenirs de Segrais et de Mongoust, *relates the poignant story of the demolition of the house : "He (Léonce Le Juge) died only a few days after consenting to the sale of the house at the end of December 1912. It was bought by a developer whose intention was to demolish the house, sell the wood and parcel up the land. A year later it was a 'fait accompli': not a stone or board was left of the venerated house, not a tree, nor even a seed remained of the old orchards."*

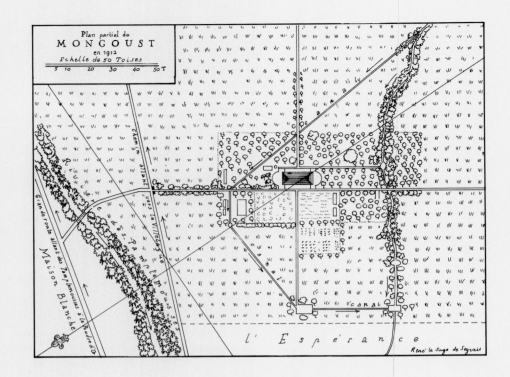

*MONGOUST
Location plan
Front elevation*

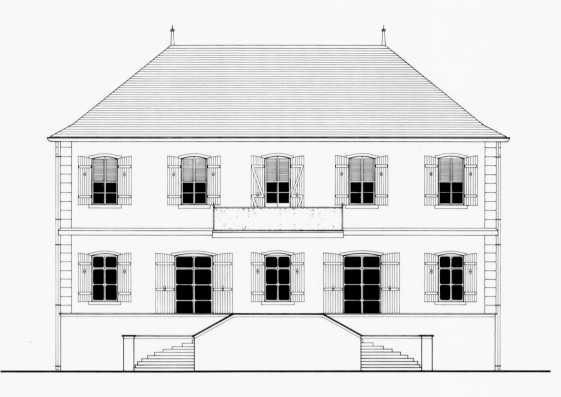

characteristics of a French abode of the XVIIIth century..." (René Le Juge de Segrais, *Souvenirs de Segrais et de Mongoust*, 1936). The houses of this period were probably built with the help of French naval carpenters whom Mahé de Labourdonnais had brought with him to build and repair ships. It is thus not surprising that the principles and techniques of naval architecture can be identified in many traditional houses.

Both houses illustrated below have roofs which can be compared to an upturned boat, the structure designed to withstand the force of the wind rather than that of water.

Even in the earliest days, shingles were used on the roofs of wooden houses. Delicate wooden slats thinned at one end were nailed onto a wooden structure. They were then covered with a thick coating of tar-based paint, comparable to that used in boat-building, which rendered them waterproof.

At that time, the development of an architectural style was taking place mainly in Port-Louis (where the town plan designed by Cossigny formed the basis for town planning). There were no villages; the settlers lived far away from one another on their plantations called *défrichés*, like islands in the middle of the vast expanse of tropical forest.

*In 1771 Jean de Robillard purchased some land and built the house that was to become the residence of successive commanders of the Grand-Port district and that is now the Mahébourg Museum. Jean de Robillard died in 1809; the following year his widow and children were to provide a refuge for the two illustrious wounded soldiers of the Battle of Grand-Port (23-26 August 1810). The French Captain Duperre and the English Captain Willoughby were cared for in the same room. The government of Mauritius acquired the house in 1947. It was transformed into a naval and historic museum and was opened to the public on 1 September 1950.*

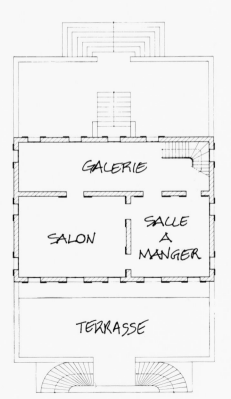

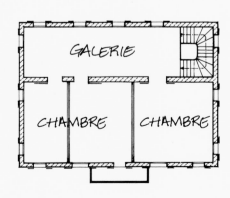

*MAHEBOURG MUSEUM*
*(the historic house of Grand Port)*
*Front elevation*
*Plan*

GALERIE

SALON

SALLE A MANGER

TERRASSE

GALERIE

CHAMBRE

CHAMBRE

# THE BIRTH OF MAURITIAN STYLE 1820-1860

By the beginning of the nineteenth century French and English settlers had realised that they should adapt their architecture to the climatic and social conditions of the tropics. All buildings from then on followed a certain number of established rules. Houses were generally made of wood on a stone foundation, the latter shielding the wooden structure from direct contact with the ground and helping with the ventilation. Their height also gave them a commanding position. Stone was generally reserved for administrative buildings and wood was used for residential purposes (the former being very difficult to use; furthermore, local mortar was not easy to mix).

The standard plan is very simple, with all rooms inter-communicating. The living room often occupies the whole depth of the house. Windows are replaced by doors, usually placed on the same axis for easier cross-ventilation.

The main building contains the living room, dining room and bedrooms. The kitchen and bathrooms are normally separate structures at the back of the house. Small pavilions were often found in the garden with additional bedrooms to cater for the larger families and their frequent guests.

Around the main structure is the verandah, an independent feature which runs on one or more sides of the house. The roof of the verandah is flat and commonly known as "argamasse", from the Portuguese word *argamassa* denoting a cement made from crushed tiles and lime. In Mauritius the recipe of argamasse was more complicated and apparently contained, apart from lime, a mixture of eggs, sugar and other exotic ingredients. This paste, perfected by the Indian craftsmen, was so hard that it was very resistant to water and lasted a long time. However, argamasse was soon to be replaced by corrugated iron.

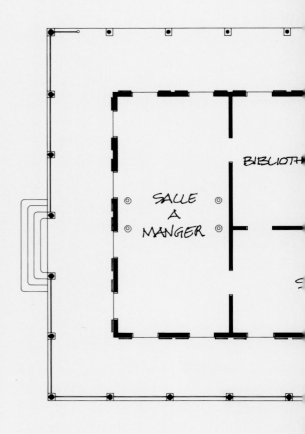

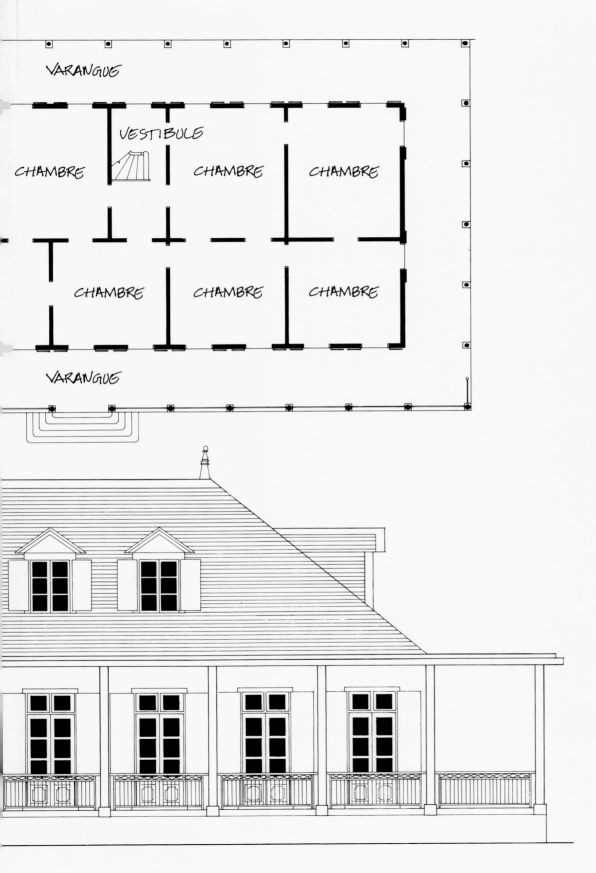

VARANGUE

VESTIBULE

CHAMBRE CHAMBRE CHAMBRE

CHAMBRE CHAMBRE CHAMBRE

VARANGUE

The verandah insulates the main body of the building: it prevents the sun from shining directly into the house and keeps the rain at bay. Furthermore, it solves the problem of communication since it provides direct access to the main rooms of the house. The verandah is a pleasant place to be at all times of the day and is normally the coolest and best lit part of the house, since the rooms are permanently plunged in semi-obscurity. In a country where hospitality is a way of life it becomes an important social feature : "...It is at the same time a noble entrance to the house, a porch... and a place of leisure for rest and social small talk..." (Preliminary studies on traditional housing in Reunion Island)

Nobody would pretend that the verandah is a Mauritian invention. It exists under various other names all over the world - "galerie", "piazza", "porch" - and epitomises a way of life for Europeans who settled abroad. In Mauritius, it is interesting to note that the inclusion of verandahs in residential designs became widespread under the British occupation which began in 1810, and this would seem to indicate the influence of other British colonies.

One could say that the verandah is the most typical feature of the Mauritian house. For those living in the tropics it is as important as is the hearth to those in the northern hemisphere.

*EUREKA*
*Plan and front elevation*
*Built in 1830 by Mr Carr, it was*
*bought by Mr Eugène LeClézio in*
*1856, and remained the property of*
*his family until February 1985.*
*Originally its grounds covered 225*
*acres of garden and forest, but they*
*are now reduced to 5 acres.*

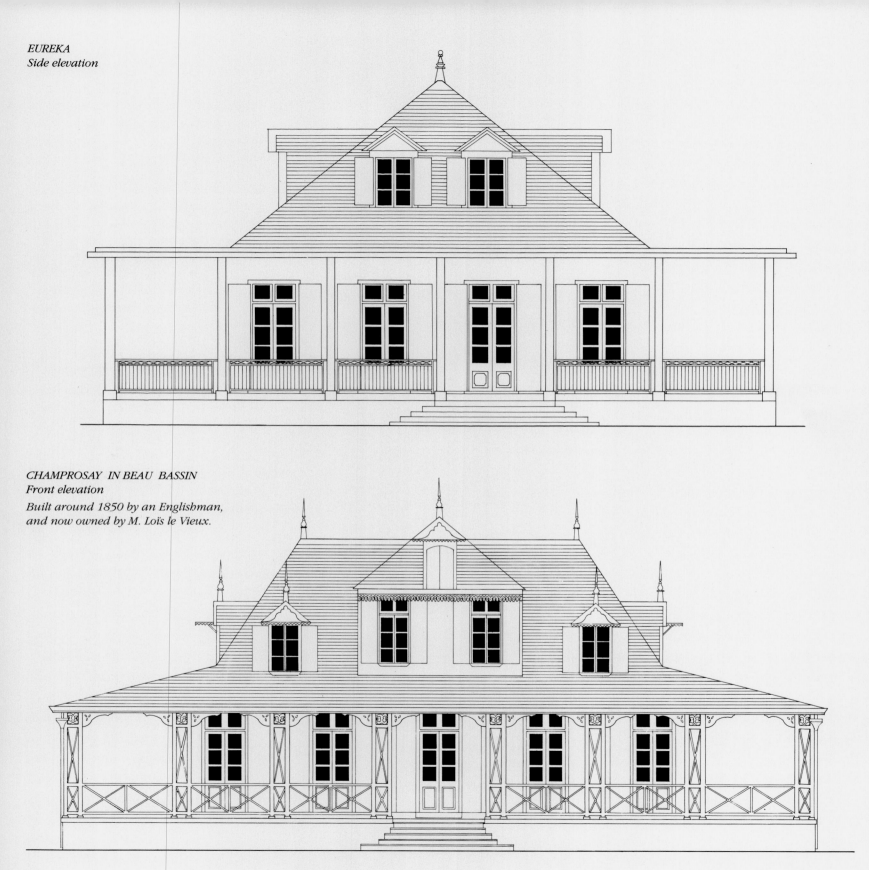

*EUREKA*
*Side elevation*

*CHAMPROSAY IN BEAU BASSIN*
*Front elevation*

*Built around 1850 by an Englishman,*
*and now owned by M. Loïs le Vieux.*

196

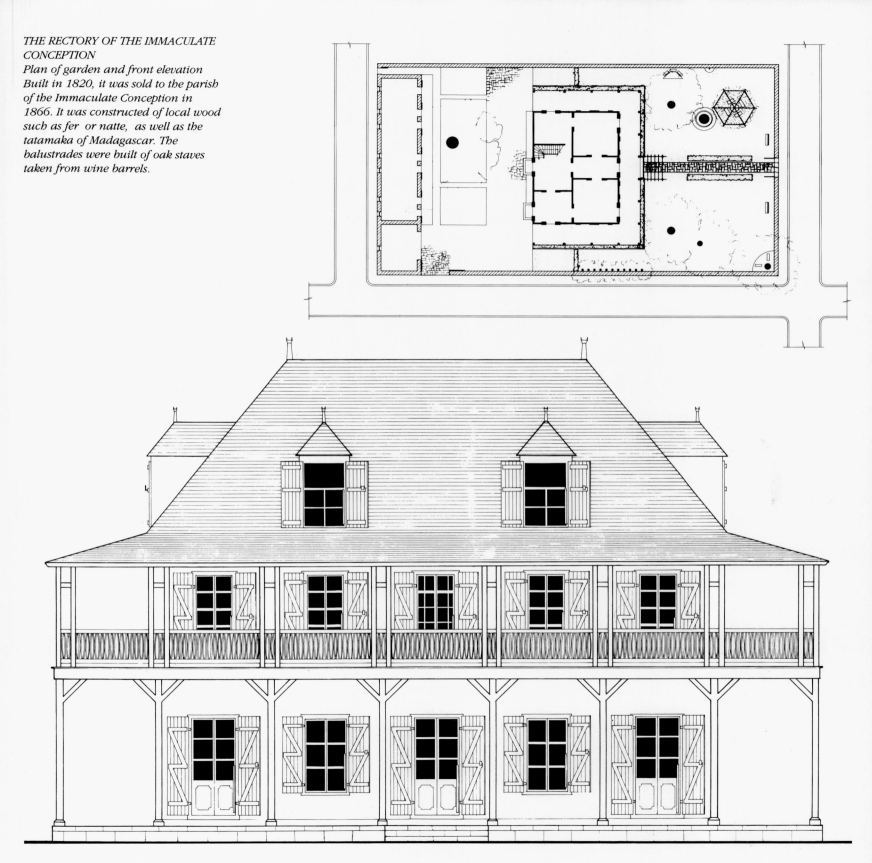

THE RECTORY OF THE IMMACULATE CONCEPTION

Plan of garden and front elevation
Built in 1820, it was sold to the parish of the Immaculate Conception in 1866. It was constructed of local wood such as fer or natte, as well as the tatamaka of Madagascar. The balustrades were built of oak staves taken from wine barrels.

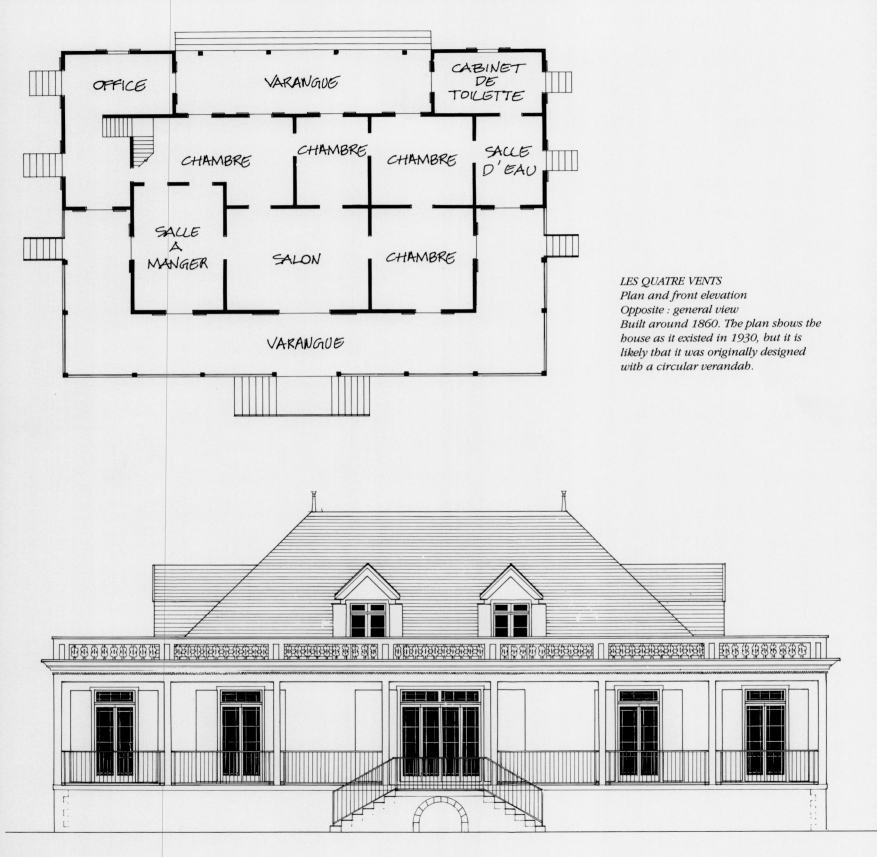

OFFICE

VARANGUE

CABINET DE TOILETTE

CHAMBRE

CHAMBRE

CHAMBRE

SALLE D'EAU

SALLE A MANGER

SALON

CHAMBRE

VARANGUE

*LES QUATRE VENTS*
*Plan and front elevation*
*Opposite : general view*
*Built around 1860. The plan shows the house as it existed in 1930, but it is likely that it was originally designed with a circular verandah.*

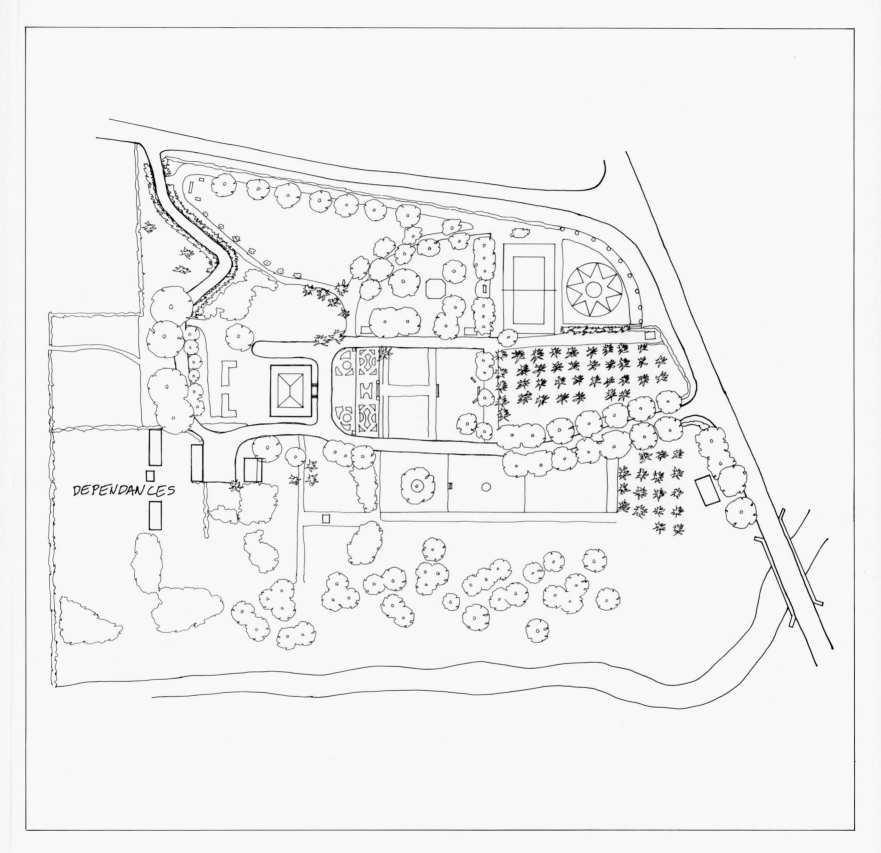

DEPENDANCES

199

# THE ROMANTIC YEARS 1860-1930

The malaria epidemics which coincided with the opening of the railways drove many families to leave Port-Louis for the healthier climate of the central plateau.

A whole series of towns and villages of residential nature gradually took shape with the railways providing a much-improved means of transport for building materials. Although many inhabitants dismantled their houses and rebuilt them on the highlands, Port-Louis remained the commercial and administrative centre.

Having mastered the techniques of the Mauritian style, the settlers could now afford to give free rein to their imagination. Thus, the romantic years saw the introduction of glazed verandahs, a multitude of roof silhouettes, turrets, windows with auvents, bow windows and, overall, an abundance of fanciful decoration.

This was a far cry from those first houses made of rough wooden planks. Not only did the house have to be comfortable but it also had to reflect the social status of its owner: the front façade and, therefore, the verandah were of utmost importance.

There are three distinct styles of verandahs : the verandah with large colonnades, the verandah with balustrades and more complex designs and decorations (these two styles often being seen together) and, finally, the glazed verandah. The latter is found in all parts of the island and even on the cooler upper plains, which would lead us to suppose that it was a social phenomenon rather than a result of climatic conditions.

*SURPRISE IN MOKA*
*Front elevation and plan*
*The main core of the house probably dates from before 1865. The turrets and the glazed verandah were subsequent additions.*

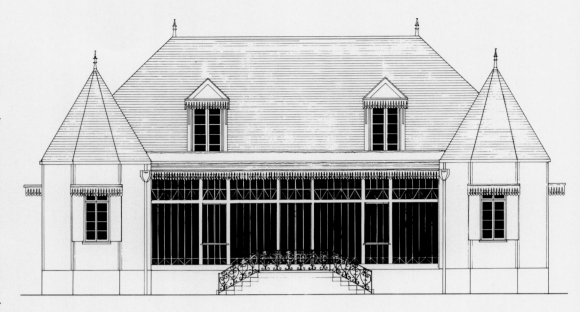

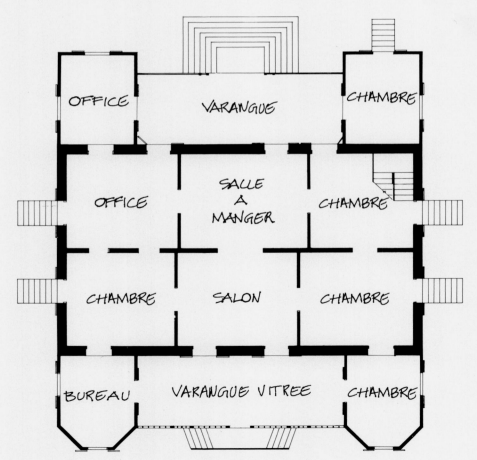

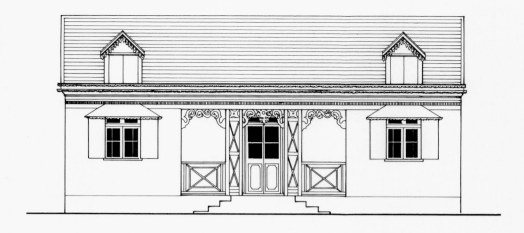

This was the era of Victorian exuberance, and of the bourgeois villas of nineteenth century France. Under British rule, the franco-Mauritian population was able to maintain its traditions and, yet, no one can be certain of the origin of any particular feature. For example, the glazed verandah could well be a version of the English conservatory which was very much in fashion in the nineteenth century, but it is equally true that the *jardin d'hiver* existed at the same time in France.

A major change which took place at that time was the shape of the roof. The hipped roof that covered all the rooms like the hull of an upturned boat was replaced by a whole series of smaller roofs, usually gabled. Here, there is a parallel with Caribbean architecture. The hipped roof is found only in the French West Indies. This would suggest that the introduction of multiple roof silhouettes was the result of British influence.

During this period the rigour and simplicity that characterised early houses were replaced by a more elaborate and complex form of architecture that was, nonetheless, based on the earlier model. There was greater freedom to create and innovate according to one's whims and fancies.

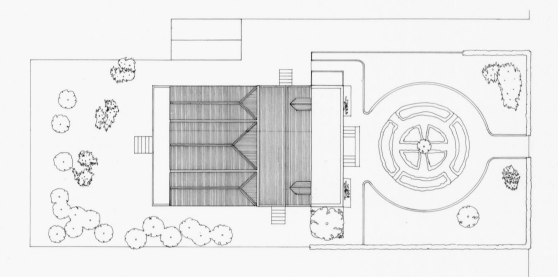

*HOUSE IN ST JULIEN D'HOTMAN*
*Front elevation and plan of the garden*
*The date of construction is unknown*
*but it is likely to have been built at the*
*turn of the century.*

*HOUSE AT LE REDUIT*
*Front elevation*
*Built in 1908 on government orders*
*with funds given by the sugar*
*industry. It was to house one of the*
*research workers from the*
*bacteriological laboratory that was*
*built at the same time.*

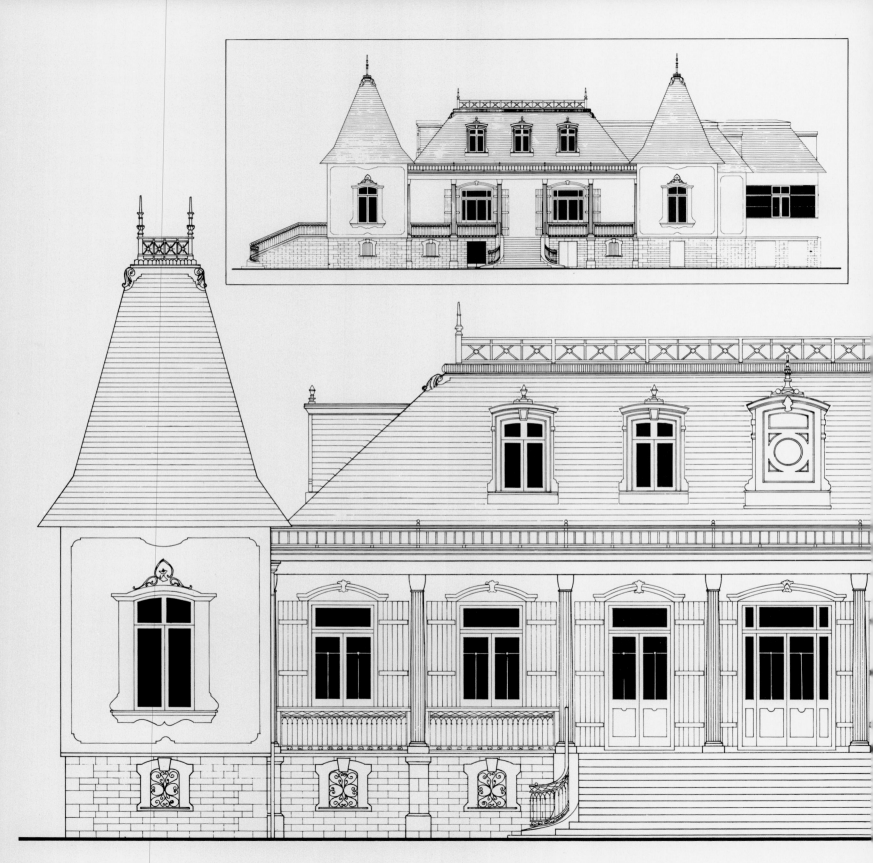

202

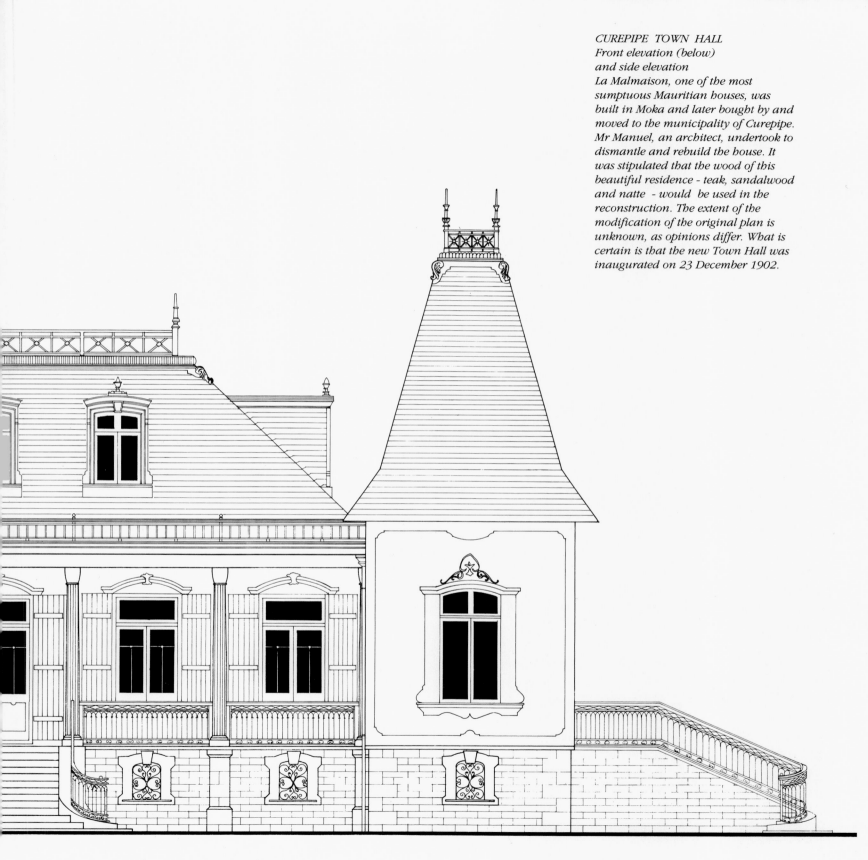

CUREPIPE TOWN HALL
*Front elevation (below)*
*and side elevation*
*La Malmaison, one of the most*
*sumptuous Mauritian houses, was*
*built in Moka and later bought by and*
*moved to the municipality of Curepipe.*
*Mr Manuel, an architect, undertook to*
*dismantle and rebuild the house. It*
*was stipulated that the wood of this*
*beautiful residence - teak, sandalwood*
*and natte - would be used in the*
*reconstruction. The extent of the*
*modification of the original plan is*
*unknown, as opinions differ. What is*
*certain is that the new Town Hall was*
*inaugurated on 23 December 1902.*

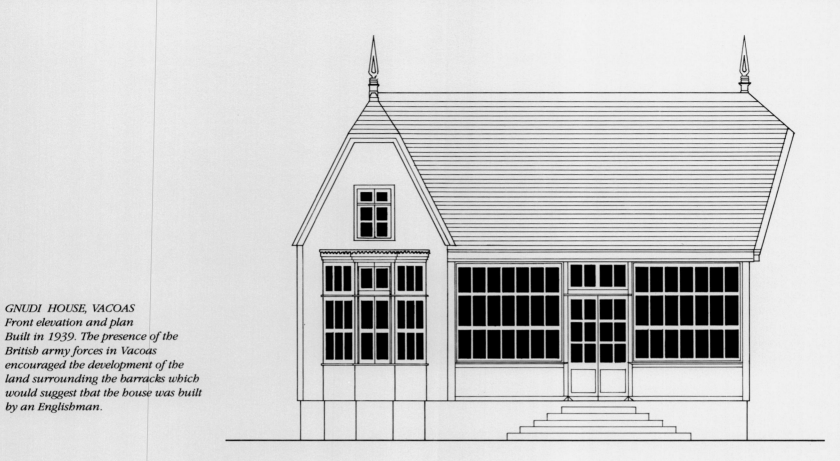

GNUDI HOUSE, VACOAS
Front elevation and plan
Built in 1939. The presence of the
British army forces in Vacoas
encouraged the development of the
land surrounding the barracks which
would suggest that the house was built
by an Englishman.

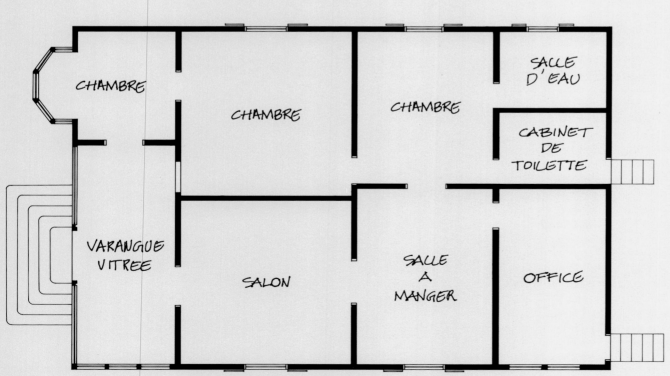

CHAMBRE

CHAMBRE

CHAMBRE

SALLE
D'EAU

CABINET
DE
TOILETTE

VARANGUE
VITREE

SALON

SALLE
A
MANGER

OFFICE

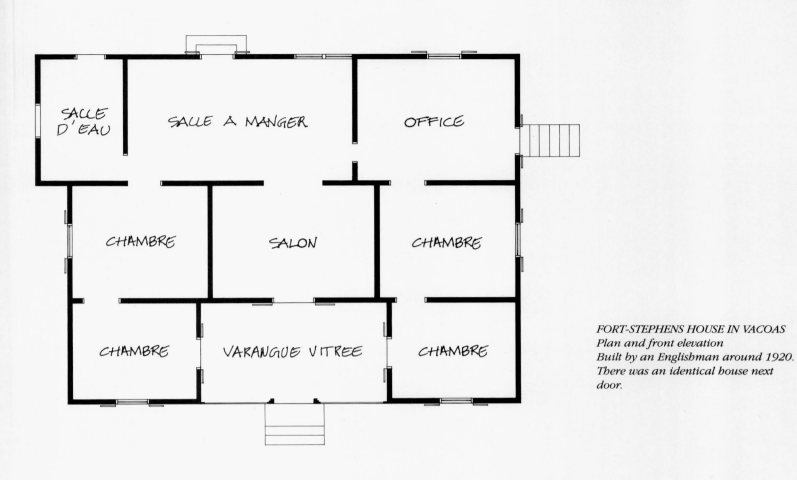

SALLE D'EAU

SALLE A MANGER

OFFICE

CHAMBRE

SALON

CHAMBRE

CHAMBRE

VARANGUE VITREE

CHAMBRE

*FORT-STEPHENS HOUSE IN VACOAS*
*Plan and front elevation*
*Built by an Englishman around 1920.*
*There was an identical house next*
*door.*

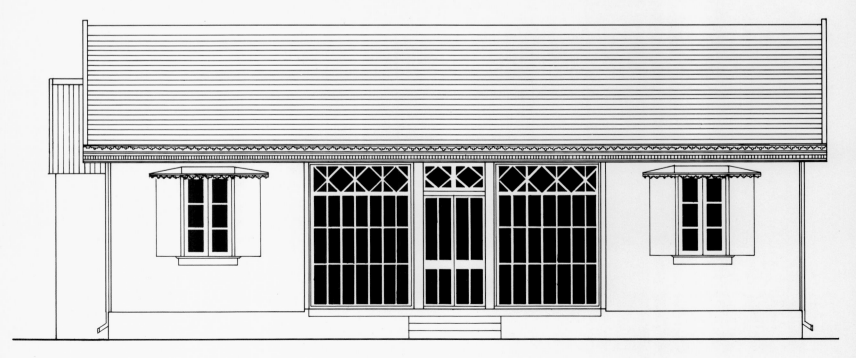

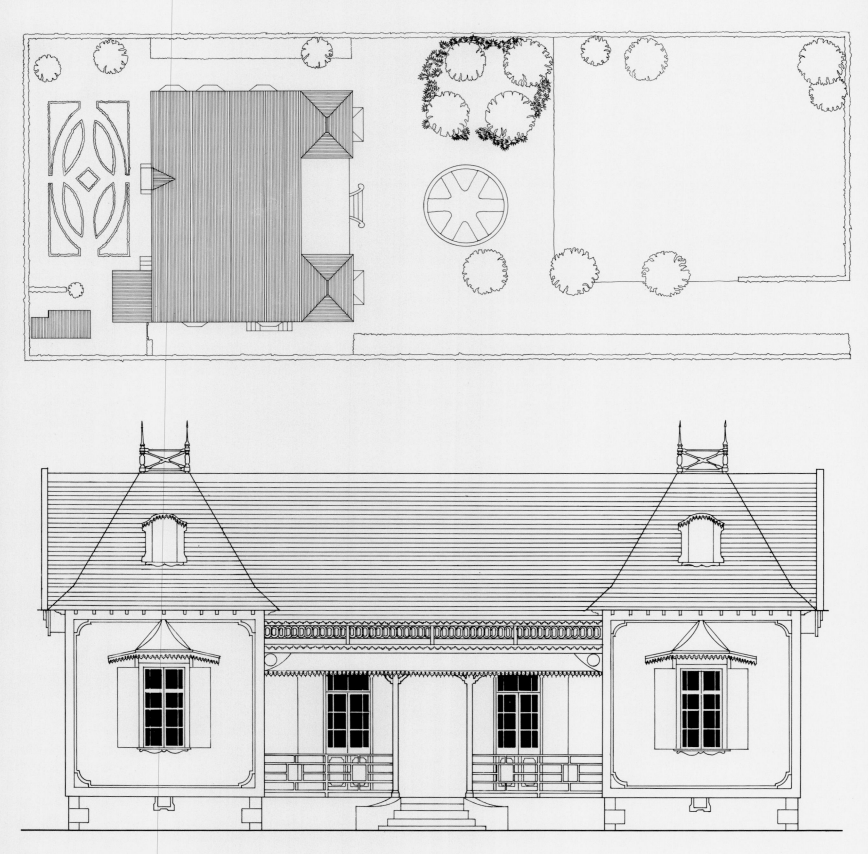

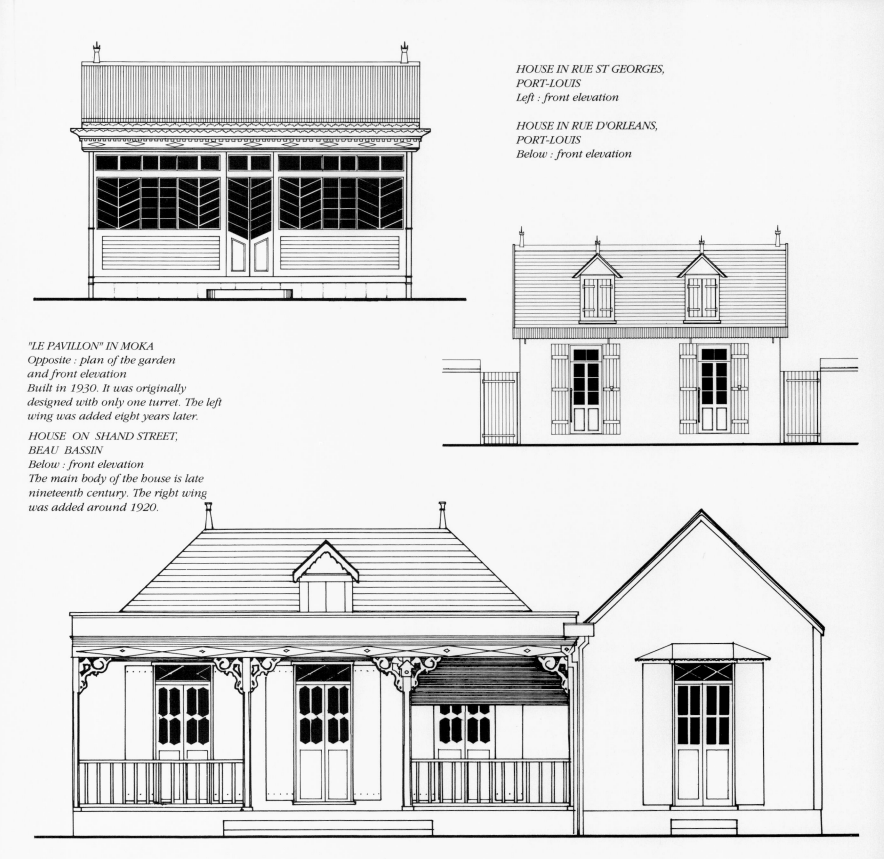

HOUSE IN RUE ST GEORGES,
PORT-LOUIS
Left : front elevation

HOUSE IN RUE D'ORLEANS,
PORT-LOUIS
Below : front elevation

"LE PAVILLON" IN MOKA
Opposite : plan of the garden
and front elevation
Built in 1930. It was originally
designed with only one turret. The left
wing was added eight years later.

HOUSE ON SHAND STREET,
BEAU BASSIN
Below : front elevation
The main body of the house is late
nineteenth century. The right wing
was added around 1920.

207

# THE LAST BASTION OF CHARACTER 1930-1960

Alas, with the growing popularity of concrete as a building material, wooden architecture gradually fell into disfavour and would have completely disappeared were it not for the popular dwelling.

Compared, to the grander residences, its proportions are modest. Nonetheless, it features all the elements of Mauritian style. In particular, there are three characteristics which help to place it in a category of its own: firstly, corrugated iron is essential; secondly, the classical colours are replaced by vivid shades which reflect the Mauritian love of "Chazalian" colours; and, lastly, the strong symmetry of the large houses is not necessarily respected. The end result is often more picturesque than that of the more imposing counterparts.

In spite of its small size, the verandah is still used as the reception area and thus becomes the heart of the house, where people actually live. The bedrooms are generally arranged symmetrically and laterally in relation to the verandah.

The kitchen is usually situated at the rear of the house in a separate structure, just as in the large houses of yesteryear.

The traditional houses of Mauritius are fast disappearing; their survival is threatened by unrestrained urban culture. Let us hope that this book will help in rallying the whole population of Mauritius to preserve this invaluable part of its national heritage. At a time when environment is a subject of public concern, we sincerely hope that the authorities will not hesitate to adopt any new legislation that will stop the process of destruction : "...for a house that has braved the ages commands our respect. It captivates our soul..." (Jean-Louis Pagès, *Maisons traditionnelles de l'Ile Maurice*)

*HOUSE IN MELROSE*
*Front elevation and plan*
*Built in 1958 by the Woozeer family.*

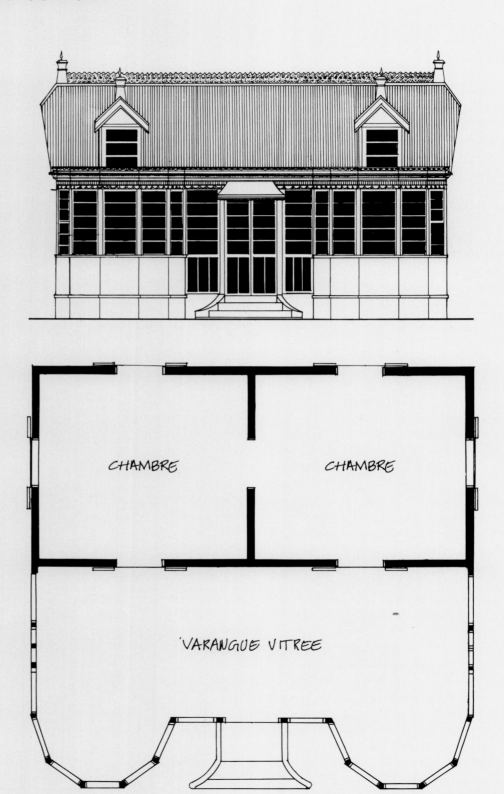

CHAMBRE

CHAMBRE

VARANGUE VITREE

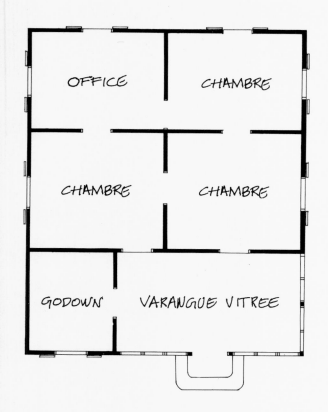

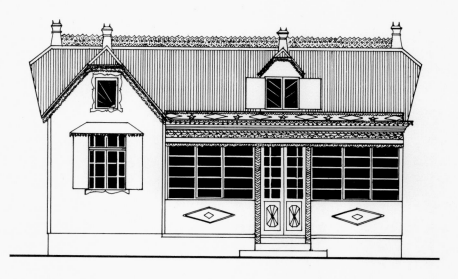

HOUSE IN TROU D'EAU DOUCE
*Above : front elevation and plan*
*Built in 1958 by Mr Beejmohun.*
*Seriously damaged by Cyclone*
*Firinga (28 January 1989), the house*
*is scheduled for demolition.*

HOUSE IN OLIVIA
*Below : front elevation*
*Built around 1950 by Mr Patpur and*
*still occupied by the same family.*

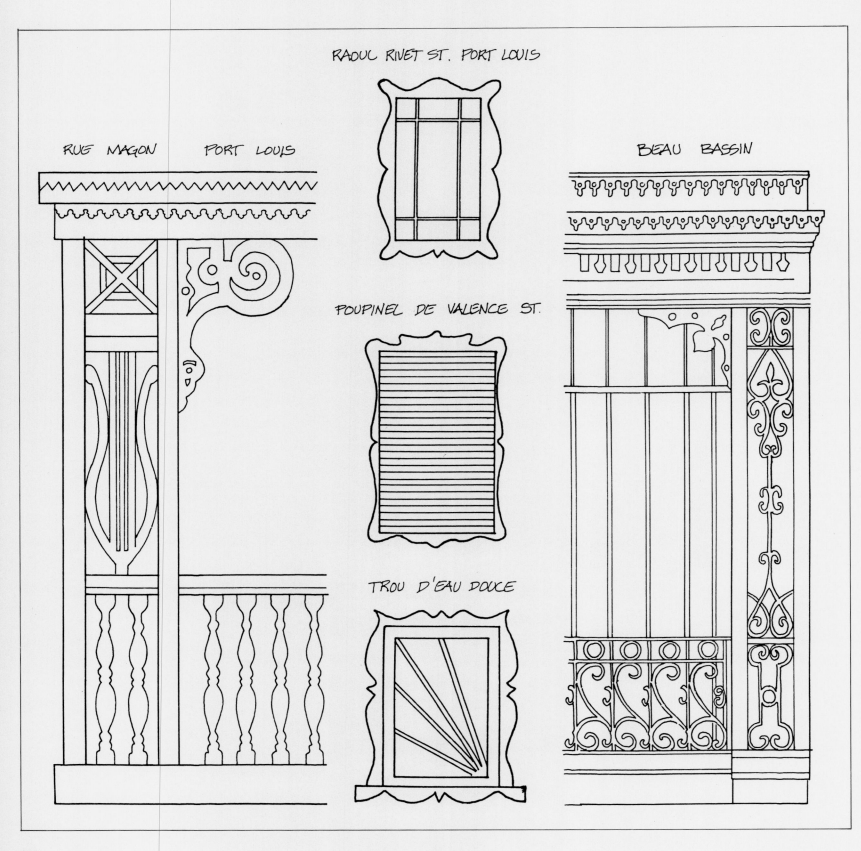

RUE MAGON    PORT LOUIS

RAOUL RIVET ST. PORT LOUIS

BEAU BASSIN

POUPINEL DE VALENCE ST.

TROU D'EAU DOUCE

210

FRISES      SEBASTOPOL      FRISES

RUE DU SOUFFLEUR.      BEAU BASSIN

LABOURDONNAIS      MON REVE

# MAURITIUS

MAURICIA

LA VILLEBAGUE

PORT LOUIS

EUREKA

COUR SUPREME DE FLACQ

MAISON LEVIEUX

CHATEAU TROMPETTE

HEADQUARTERS HOUSE

MAISON GUIMBEAU

RICHE EN EAU

MUSEE DE MAHEBOURG

BEL OMBRE

ST AUBIN

# GLOSSARY

**Argamasse**: usually refers to the flat roof of the verandah; also refers to the mixture used to coat these roofs. There are numerous recipes for this mixture. Lime is the basic ingredient, but a surprising variety of other ingredients may be added.

**Auvent**: an overlang or canopy above a door or window; it protects the interior from both sun and rain.

**Boutique**: general grocery shop, usually owned and run by the Chinese.

**Campement**: a typical Mauritian term for a seaside bungalow. Originally applied only to the ravenala huts where families spent the summer months, the term is now used to describe any modern seaside cottage.

**Case**: a small house, or cabin, usually made of wood.

**Chalis**: polished cement floor used on the verandah and within the house and usually painted red.

**Chassé**: private land given over to deer hunting.

**Chazal, Malcolm de (1902-1981)**: a Mauritian naïve painter.

**Défriché**: a plantation, literally an area of tropical forest that has been cleared.

**Jardin d'hiver**: literally winter garden, but comparable to a conservatory.

**Ravenala**: the central veins of the ravenala leaf are used in the construction of campements. The ravenala, popularly known as "travellers tree" originates from Madagascar.

**Roche carri**: cut stone on which spices are crushed. An indispensable part of the kitchen in any Mauritian home.

**Season**: winter months traditionally spent at the seaside.

**Upper plateau**: rising steeply from the coast, the elevation of the plateau varies from 200 to 700 metres; its coolness is much appreciated during the summer months.

# BIBLIOGRAPHY

## HISTORY

ADOLPHE Harold and LAGESSE Marcelle, *L'Hôtel du Gouvernement* (1973)

BARNWELL P.J., *Visits and Despatches 1598-1948* (1948)

DE SORNAY Pierre, *Isle de France, Ile Maurice* (1950)

DUCRAY C.G., *Histoire de la ville de Curepipe, notes et anecdotes* (1941)

FELIX J.E., *The Historical Monuments of Mauritius*, Colony of Mauritius, Education Department (1958)

JERNINGHAM H.E.H. GMG Lieut. Governor of Mauritius and Dependencies, "Cyclone of April 29th in Mauritius, 1892", *Pamphlets*, volume 124 (1892)

JESSOP A., *A History of the Mauritius Government Railways 1864-1964* (1964)

LAGESSE Marcelle, "La recette de l'Argamasse", *La gazette des îles de la mer des Indes* (January 1987)

LE JUGE DE SEGRAIS R., *Souvenir de Segrais de Mongoust* (1936)

MACMILLAN Allister, *Mauritius illustrated – historical and descriptive, commercial and industrial facts, figures and resources*, WH & L Collinbridge, London (1914)

NEWTON Robert, *Le Réduit 1748-1960* (1960)

PAGES J-L., *Maisons traditionnelles de l'Île Maurice*, Éditions de l'Océan Indien, Île Maurice (1978)

ROUILLARD G., *Histoire des Domaines sucriers de l'Île Maurice*, The General Printing and Stationary Co Ltd, Mauritius (1964-79)

TOUSSAINT A., *Port Louis, deux siècles d'histoires 1735-1935*, La Typographie Moderne, Port-Louis (1936)

## ECONOMY AND GEOGRAPHY

PADYA B.M., *Cyclones of the Mauritius Region*, Met. Off. Mauritius (1976)

PATURAU Maurice, *Histoire économique de l'Île Maurice*

## TRAVEL ACCOUNTS

BARTRUM Lady A., *Recollections of seven years residence at Mauritius, or the Isle of France, by a lady* (1838)

BACKHOUSE Alexander, *A narrative of a visit to the Mauritius* (1844)

BEATON Rev. P., *Creoles and coolies: or five years in Mauritius*, Nisbet (1859)

BOYLE C.J., *Far away, or sketches of scenery and society in Mauritius* (1867)

SAINT-PIERRE Bernardin de, *Voyage à l'Ilsle de France* (1812)

MILBERT M. G., *Voyage pittoresque à l'Isle de France* (1812)

MOUAT F.J., *Rough notes of a trip to Reunion, the Mauritius and Ceylon with remarks on their eligibility for Indian Invalids*, Calcutta (1852)

*Journal of five months Residence in Mauritius by a Bengal Civilian*, Calcutta (1852).

*A late official Resident: An account of the island of Mauritius and its dependencies* (1842).

## GENERAL REFERENCES

### LA REUNION

*Études préliminaires sur l'habitat traditionnel dans le département de la Réunion*, Ministère de la Construction et de l'Urbanisme (1963)

DELCOURT J.F., *Regards sur l'architecture à St Denis, Île de la Réunion*, Direction dépt de l'Équipement, Groupe d'Études et de Programmation.

VAISSE C., HENNEQUET F., BARAT C., AUGEARD Y., *Cases cachées*, Les Éditions du Pacifique (1987)

### EUROPE

MIGNOT C., *L'architecture au XIXᵉ siècle*, Éditions du Moniteur (1983)

### AUSTRALIA

PAYNTER J., "The Australian verandah", *Architecture in Australia*, vol. 93 (June 1965)

### INDIA

KING A.D., *The Bungalow: the production of a global culture*, Routledge and Keegan Paul (1984)

POTT J., *Bungalows of Bangalore*

### WEST INDIES

SLESIN S., CLIFF S., BERTHELOT J., GAUME M., ROZENSZTROCH D., MORRIS J., CHABANEIX DE G., *L'Art de vivre aux Antilles*, Éditions Flammarion (1986)

BERTHELOT J., GAUME M., *Caribbean popular dwelling*, Exhibition Centre Georges Pompidou, Perspective Creole (1983)

EDWARDS J.D., *Cultural traditions and Caribbean identity; the question of patrimony; the evolution of vernacular architecture in the western Caribbean*, Center for Latin American Studies, University of Florida (1980)

### USA

OVERDYKE Darrel W., *Louisiana plantation houses, colonial and ante bellum*.

TOLEDANO, DITTREDGE EVANS, CHRISTOVITCH, "The creole faubourgs. History by Samuel Wilson Jnr", *New Orleans Architecture*, vol IV, Pelican Publishing Co., Gretna (1974).

## THESES, UNPUBLISHED DOCUMENTS

DESMARAIS Pierre, *A study of colonial houses in Mauritius* (1960)

DESVAUX DE MARIGNY Isabelle, *The colonial house in Mauritius* (1980)

LAGESSE Henriette, *The traditional colonial architecture of Mauritius*, Cambridge University (1986)

LAGESSE Pierre, *The creole house of Mauritius 1730-1890*, Cambridge University (1959)

## ACKNOWLEDGEMENTS

We would like to thank all those who offered advice, enthusiasm and the permission for their houses to be included in this book. Special thanks to Guy Rouillard, Maurice Paturau, Jean-François Desvaux de Marigny, Philippe Valentin, Pierre Lagesse, Bernard Boullé for his help in translation, Tristan Bréville for the loan of photographs from the Museum of Photography, Guillemette de Spéville for her documents concerning Malcolm de Chazal, Marc Daruty de Grandpré for his drawings of Curepipe Town Hall and Guido A Rossi for the aerial photograph on page 63. Thanks also to Air Mauritius, the Ministries of Education and Tourism, and the hotel chains, Beachcomber, Sun International, Hotel PLM Méridien and Club Méditerannée. The photographer is especially grateful to Jacqueline Rabot for her invaluable help and advice.

All the exterior photographs were taken on Kodachrome 64 ASA and the interior ones on Ektachrome 100 ASA. The photographer used Nikon equipment.